ALL OUR STORIES

MEMORIES OF WEST MALLING AND ITS VILLAGES

All Our Sories

Paperback edition ISBN: 978-0-9927658-0-4
eBook edition ISBN: 978-0-9927658-1-1

Layout design by Ali Scrivens, TJGraphics

Cover design by Michael Rowe MBE JP

Published by The Beat Project

10 Park Road, Sittingbourne, Kent ME10 1DR

www.thebeatproject.org.uk

Printed by Orbital Print Limited. www.orbitalprint.co.uk

Second edition, December 2013

Owing to the age of some of the photographs, the reproduction is affected.

Disclaimer

CONTENTS

INTRODUCTION

The idea of 'All Our Stories' came about through an already established partnership between the Malling Action Partnership and a local community development charity, The Beat Project.

The partnership acknowledged that, whilst many local people feel passionately about the history and heritage of this area, there are concerns that the memories of people who have lived through and experienced significant events in the recent past are being lost, as they reach the end of their lives. They also felt that very little heritage work has been done in the West Malling area and there is a lack of such resources available to the local community. The production of a book and online resource would, therefore, be a valuable asset for current and future generations.

Trudy Dean, County Councillor, Chair of West Malling Parish Council and Chair of the Malling Action Partnership tells the story of her motivation to bring this project to fruition...

"A dear friend of ours, Percy Macey, who was very important to the local community in all sorts of ways, mainly with young people and sport – he facilitated all sorts of things, for the football teams particularly, and he was a founder member of the village hall, and he was a member of the Parish Council, and what there was to be known about West Malling - he knew it! We named our Community Orchard after him...Macey's Meadow.
He wasn't particularly old but one day I said to him, 'You should get all of this recorded', because at that time the Malling Society were doing recordings. And he said, 'Oh no, I could never sit with a tape recorder.' And I said, 'What you just need to do is sit and chat to somebody, you know, in front of the fire.' And he said, 'Oh, I think I could do that,' and then of course I didn't do anything about it, and he died shortly afterwards, unexpectedly. I thought, 'We mustn't miss these opportunities, they're just gold.'
So that was one of the reasons why when we started talking about the project, I was so keen."

The Beat Project successfully bid for a Heritage Lottery Fund grant and the rest is history, as they say!

This book was, therefore, made possible through the Heritage Lottery Fund 'All Our Stories' Grant Scheme. It is part of the 'Capturing Community Heritage in the West Malling area' project comprising an online book and website featuring personal recollections of local people in the area through photographs, film and audio. It records the history and heritage through the memories of local people living in West Malling, Addington, Birling, East Malling, Kings Hill, Larkfield, Leybourne, Mereworth, Offham, Ryarsh and Trottiscliffe.

'All Our Stories' began early in 2013 with the formation of a 'Community Heritage Panel'. The panel has steered the project forward and members have helped with all aspects. They have provided contacts, helped at workshops, undertaken historical research, collated the stories for, and even helped design the book. They have told their own stories and brought their extensive local knowledge to the project.

A Community Heritage Workshop was held in each parish in the spring of 2013, enabling local people to contribute. Many people were filmed talking about their memories at the workshops and others came to learn more about their local area, or to contribute photos and stories to the project. Rachael Carley, from the Beat Project, and Leader of 'All our Stories', also visited local schools and care homes, and interviewed the people who were unable to reach the workshops, in their own homes. In total, over 60 people contributed stories and memories - a further 200, plus schools and local organisations, were involved through the workshops, or by supporting the project in other ways.

THE COMMUNITY HERITAGE PANEL

Andrew Wells

Andrew Wells is an architectural historian who lectures on historic buildings and leads related tours. He holds an MA in the architecture and history of country houses and has written the guidebook to Mereworth's Grade I Palladian church, where he was a churchwarden for seven years. He is a member of the Kent Historic Buildings Committee, a former Chairman of the SE Region of the Historic Houses Association, and was High Sheriff of Kent in 2005-6. His family has lived in west Kent since the early 17th century and at Mereworth for over 50 years. His maternal links with the village go back to the middle ages.

Bernard Tyson

Bernard Tyson is married to Anne with three children and has lived in Kent since 1962. After finishing National Service he joined the family shipping and travel firm, is a Chartered Shipbroker and has served on several travel trade committees. He moved to West Malling in 1983 and has been Chairman of the Malling Society for over 20 years. He is a Trustee of the Malling Memorial Institute (the Clout), committee member of the Malling Action Partnership, served on the Quality Co-ordinating Circle at Maidstone Hospital, and has been Chairman of the Cardiac Support Group at the Hospital. Bernard has been the Kent Messenger, West Malling Village Correspondent for over 20 years.

Christine Woodger

Christine is a Parish and Borough Councillor and lives in Well Street, East Malling in a Medieval Hall House built in 1410 by John Derby. Her husband's family has a long history in the area - in the 1911 census there were seventeen Woodgers living in Well Street. When Christine moved to East Malling she recalls that Miss Martin in Broadwater still put out milk churns at the side of the road for collection. Her house was later demolished and Broadwater Hall was built on its site. Hops were also still grown in the field opposite Christine's house and the hops were dried in the oast houses. Christine recalls that one evening a scout committee meeting was held in the oast house at Heath farm as the farmer could not leave the hops unattended. The very pungent smell of the hops permeated her clothes for ages! Christine worked for many years at St James School and is now a Trustee of the St James Centre Trust.

David Fillery

David moved to Leybourne twenty years ago having lived for the previous twenty eight years, six miles away in Barming. David has recently been writing his family history and joined the Community Heritage Panel as a representative for Leybourne.

He was previously Chairman of the LEYARA (Leybourne Active Retirement Association).

David Thornewell

David was born in 1948. He has lived in Larkfield all his life and went to the old Church of England Primary School (next to the Church in New Hythe Lane) before going to Aylesford Secondary School followed by Mid Kent College, Maidstone. His mother was Mavis Brimsted - the Brimsteds having lived in the area for at least the last 200 years.

Until retirement, David was a Legal Executive working for local solicitors in Maidstone.

He served on the old Malling Rural District Council for the last two years of its existence - from 1972 to 1974. He was then a Tonbridge and Malling Borough Councillor for Larkfield from 1974 to 2011, being Council Leader from 1995 to 2003. He was made a Freeman of the Borough in March 2012.

David has also been a Larkfield Parish Councillor since 1969 and is currently Chairman. He is interested in local history and is a keen walker - often leading walks for the council and the local Ramblers Association.

Linda Javens (nee Gandon)

Linda was born in 1942. Her family have a long history in the area, having resided in West Malling for well over 100 years. Her great-grandparents ran 'The Wheatsheaf' public house in the early 1890s before running a shop in the New Town area of West Malling. Her great grandfather also worked as the local undertaker until the early 1900s. Linda's parents were very active in the local community. Her father Dennis, known as Fred, was an active member of the West Malling Parish Council and worked tirelessly to give West Malling its village hall.

Linda attended Leybourne School before going on to Snodland Secondary School, where she was Head Girl. She has lived locally all her life and worked at Reeds and Leybourne Grange Hospital. She was a founder member of SWAG – an organisation that campaigned against the developments at Kings Hill and a founder member of the local branch of the Royal Air Force Association.

Margaret Ivell JP

Margaret Ivell, born 1936, has a long family history in Birling. Her grandparents on both sides of the family settled in Birling in the late eighteenth to early twentieth century and worked at Birling Manor. Margaret has playing an active role in village life as well as the wider community – through the village hall committee and through her service to the church in Birling - where she is involved in the organisation of the highly regarded annual Flower Festival. Margaret is also involved in a range of charity work and was a magistrate for many years. She has a keen interest in local history and has been an avid movie goer from a young age.

Michael D Rowe MBE JP

Mike was born in 1942 in the city of York and is proud to be a Yorkshireman. He was educated at Birmingham University graduating with a degree in Mechanical Engineering. He became a Chartered Engineer and spent over 30 years in the electricity supply industry working on nuclear power. He was a Kent magistrate for 30 years and some time Chairman of the Central Kent Bench. He was made MBE in 2004 for services to Malling Citizens Advice Bureau (Chairman of the Trustee Board). He is a founder member of the Offham Society and is currently its Chairman. Mike has lived in Offham since 1975 and has a keen interest in local history. Mike also leads the Malling U3A Digital Photography Group.

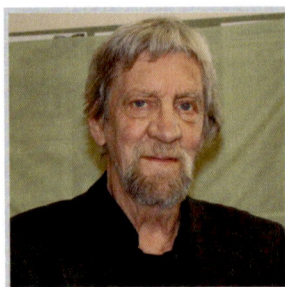

Mike North

Mike was born in 1940 at Hitchin, Hertfordshire. He has lived in West Malling for twenty years and is a Vice Chairman of the Malling Society. Mike also serves on the Parish Council Planning Committee and is a guide and lecturer on historic buildings, archaeology and landscape studies. Mike attended Sidcup School of Art before studying for a BA Hons in Kent History & Archaeology and then an MA in Medieval Architecture. He has worked as a commercial artist, professional musician, geophysical survey analyst and antique dealer. In his spare time he restores and maintains his collection of vintage cars, and surveys / researches the local historic buildings of the area.

Molly Potts

Molly came to West Malling from Bexleyheath in June 1966. She started work at Douces Manor in 1972, worked there for many years and researched its history. Having had a lifelong interest in history she joined the Malling Society soon after arriving in the area. She helped to clean off all the glass negatives from the Freda Barton Collection (Freda Barton was a commercial photographer in West Malling from the late 1890s until WWII. Her glass negatives were discovered acting as cloches in a vegetable patch – dirty but fortunately, unharmed). Molly remains involved in Douces Manor and can often be found at the Open Days at the Twitch Inn Heritage Centre. The Twitch Inn was a small pub used by the RAF during World War II and is now owned and managed by The Malling Society.

Patricia Richardson

Patricia came to live in Addington with her husband and three young children in 1976. During the 1980's and 1990's, she was a parish councillor. During this time, she served a three year term as Chairman of the Kent Association of Parish Councils. She has also been a member of two housing associations, the Kent Probation Board and the Maidstone Community Health Council. She became interested in the history of her village and researched its people and past in depth. Having retired from community service she wrote and published Addington's first full history in 2012. Patricia also wrote the parish history sections for Birling, Addington, Ryarsh, Trottiscliffe and Leybourne, as well as researching the background facts and information to many stories in this book.

Rachael Carley

Rachael founded The Beat Project with her husband, Steve, in 2002 and has worked for the organisation since that time. Rachael has many years' experience running youth and community projects and, whilst she is usually found working behind the scenes, her interest in social history prompted her to lead the 'All Our Stories'project. Rachael currently lives in East Kent with her family where she pursues her hobbies and interests in architecture, design, personal development and the great outdoors.

Roger Roud

Roger moved to East Malling in 1977 from Bexley to 'escape to the country'. He worked at Trebor Sharpe at Maidstone as an industrial engineer for 14 years, before moving into the haulage industry until retirement in 2012. He has an interest in local and family history so joined East Malling Conservation Group and looked after the archives for the group before taking on the role of Chairman eighteen months ago. Roger has also served on the committee of the East Malling Institute Trust for the past five years and is motorbike enthusiast.

CONTRIBUTORS AND THEIR STORIES

Alison Lowe and Marion Regan

Alison and her daughter Marion live at Baron's Place Farm, a major soft fruit growing farm in Mereworth. Alison was born in 1932 and moved to the area in 1957 when she married Marion's father, Hugh Lowe.

Marion was born in 1960 and now runs the farm where she carries on the family tradition of growing fruit – a tradition that started with her great grandfather, Bernard Champion, in 1892.

Ann Fisher and her mother, Mrs Ena Wickens (nee Allman)

Ann has lived in the village of Mereworth for over 50 years. Her connections go back further in that her mother, Ena Wickens nee Allman, was born in Mereworth. Ann's parents moved to Teston and Barming before returning to Mereworth when she was eight, though she has strong memories of the village from an early age due to family visits and frequent stays with one of her mother's sisters, her Aunt Kath and Uncle John (Ford). Ann married her husband, Alan, 40 years ago and moved into their present house in Kent Street.

Ena Wickens was born at 2 North Star Cottages, Butchers Lane, Mereworth in 1929. Her grandparents also lived in the village. Ena attended Mereworth Primary school and later worked at the village grocers.

Ann Kemp

Ann was born in 1941. She moved to Trottiscliffe in 1969. For forty years she ran the village playgroup in her house before it closed in 2013. Ann has immersed herself in local life and service to the community - having been a Parish Councillor for twenty years, a Borough Councillor for sixteen years, Chair of Governors - Trottiscliffe School and Mayor of Tonbridge and Malling during 2007 – 2008.

Audrey Marsh

Audrey was born in 1927, is originally from Nottingham and moved to Addington in 1964. Audrey was a teacher for many years. She became interested in the social history of Addington when she moved to the area and has developed a private exhibition focusing on 'the history of the working man'. Audrey's husband was widely involved in many aspects of life in the local area such as the Parish Council, Dramatic Society, the Church and for 23 years he was President of the cricket club. Audrey and her husband, through their work with the Lions International, were also involved in the Warbirds Airshows held on the old West Malling airfield, now home to the Kings Hill housing estate.

Audrey Reeves

Audrey has lived in Addington since 1960. She ran the village playgroup for many years and, together with Joan Scott, organised the Addington Annual Party for their senior citizens. The first annual party was organised for the 1977 Silver Jubilee and ran for about 20 years.

Barbara Earl

Barbara worked at New Scotland Yard as a civil servant before joining the police, aged nineteen, in 1973. She was one of the few local women police officers in the area and was posted to West Malling Police Station in 1974. Her main function was to deal with women and children. She also helped to set up the Juvenile Bureau in 1977. She resigned when her daughter was born in 1979 and subsequently worked as a parish clerk in the local area.

Barbara Harper

Mrs Harper moved to the area when she married her husband, Ernest Harper, who was a surgeon based at Maidstone hospital. She lived in East Malling, Addington and West Malling and had three daughters. She was a keen golfer and knitter – making many soft toys for charity – teddies that were given to children in hospitals in Africa. Mrs Harper served in the VAD during the war and remembers the Battle of Britain, treating the facial burns of pilots. She later met up with one of the pilots she had treated when she saw a newspaper article about him – he had been traced by some enthusiasts, from the engine number found on the salvage of his crashed Hurricane. Mrs Harper was awarded three Red Cross medals for her service, which are on display at The Twitch Inn – Malling Heritage Centre, Douces Manor, West Malling. Mrs Harper was born in Surrey and would have been one hundred years old in December. She sadly passed away in September 2013.

Betty Honess and Veronica Brimsted

Betty Honess (*centre*) and Veronica Brimsted (*right*) are pictured here with their friend, Ann Turner (*left*). All three ladies have lived in West Malling for many years and were, together with their families, involved in helping to raise the funds for the Village Hall. They have continued to help to run the hall since it was opened in 1975.

CONTRIBUTORS AND THEIR STORIES

Bob Clarke

Bob was born in 1938 in West Malling. He moved to Leybourne in 1939 and lived there until 2010, when he moved to East Malling. Bob had a couple of jobs locally before he started to work, aged 16, on the railways. Starting at East Malling railway station, his work took him to stations in London and all over Kent before finishing his working life at West Malling railway station, after forty two years of service.

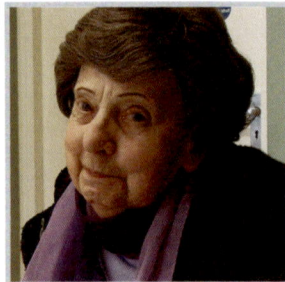

Brenda Botteril

Brenda was born in June 1929 and has lived locally all her life, as did her parents before her. She attended Ryarsh School and has dedicated much of her life to her church and local community and has raised a lot of money for the Church through the organisation of annual Art Festivals. Her husband was also greatly involved in local life and was an engineer. He once built a miniature steam train that people could ride on and he would take this to local schools and events such as Offham May Day. He also made the Ryarsh Church weather vane.

Christina Rogerson

Christina joined the team at Offham School in 1988 as Secretary and Finance Officer and has happily worked at the school ever since that time.

David Murray

David lives with his wife, Sue, and son, Luke, in Kings Hill where he settled in 1995.

David was a founder member of the Kings Hill Residents' Association and Neighbourhood Watch initiative and was one of the first members of the Kings Hill Parish Council when it formed in 1999, serving as Vice-Chair for seven years, then as Chair for a further three years.

Dave Smith

Dave was born in 1953. He grew up in Mereworth and still lives nearby. His father was a well-known local figure who ran deliveries for the village store for many years. Dave was a public servant for many years having worked in the Civil Service for the Ministry of Defence and The Ministry of Agriculture, Fisheries and Food before taking early retirement to run his own business, to raise money for charity and pursue his many hobbies and interests.

David Cameron

David was born in Bermondsey in 1926. He was evacuated to Sussex in 1939, then later went on to act as a messenger during the Blitz. He served in the Army Parachute Regiment in Palestine as a young man and on return to England, he started his own business and was to become a successful businessman. David moved from London to live in Addington in 1966 with his wife, Lily, and five daughters. He soon became involved in village life – as treasurer of the Addington Recreation Ground group. He then became involved with the village hall committee and was instrumental in setting up a PTA at nearby Wrotham School, where he was also a school Governor. In the late 1970s, David bought 'Greenways' entertainment complex in Addington – developing it into a top venue for bands, events and functions. David is currently writing his memoirs and lives in Leybourne.

Derek Brown

Derek was born in Surrey in August 1932 before moving to Snodland with his family in 1936. His father was a draper and his mother was a piano teacher. He moved to Larkfield in 1960 and worked locally for Ewbank and Partners – the company that designed and built Kingsnorth power station. Derek changed jobs so that he could remain local to see his children grow up. He therefore worked for a number of engineering consultants through the years, with his last 18 years spent working for Clark Nicholls Marcel. Derek was a regular attendee at Holy Trinity Church for many years.

(Mary Warren and) Derek Brown

Derek Stockton

Derek was born in 1928 in High Wycombe. He settled in Butchers Lane, Mereworth in 1951 and still lives there today. He raised his family in the village and worked on local farms and for other local village businesses, throughout his life.

Diane Hart

Diane has lived all her life in West Malling and she has a long family history in the area. She has been very involved in village life over the years – as a Parish Councillor and a supporter of local clubs, societies and causes.

Diz Bernal

Diz's husband, Peter, was a founder member of the East Malling Conservation Group and quickly recruited Diz as a member. Whilst Diz no longer lives within the confines of the village, she states that she is grateful for the forty years that she spent there and that, for her, East Malling will always be a very special place.

Douglas Rabjohn

Mr Rabjohn was born in a cottage in Birling near 'The Bull' public house. His family had worked at Birling Manor for many years - his father had followed his grandfather as Head Gardener there and worked there until the gardens closed. He went to school locally before serving in the Army. On his return from the war, he trained as a teacher at the primary school in East Malling, where he worked until his retirement. He was a prominent local figure, involved in many aspects of community life in East Malling – cricket, fetes, maypole dancing and many other clubs and societies.

Jean Herrington

Jean has lived in East Malling since 1956. Over the years, she has enjoyed working on the local farms in the area and has enjoyed living in the village, finding it to be a very friendly place.

Joan Bygrave

Joan is 80 years old. She moved into the village of Addington in 1966 and worked in the nursing section of the former Leybourne Grange Hospital for more than 30 years. Joan served on the local parish council in the 1980s and tried to master bell-ringing. Her interests often contain a historical edge – social history, archaeology, architecture, genealogy, though her abiding passion is family history – Joan has letters going back to the 1600's and can even prove that Bishop Stillington (1420 – 1491) was an early forbear. - Bishop Stillington was the man who put the cat amongst the pigeons by revealing that he had previously married Edward IV to Lady Eleanor Butler, before Edward decided to wed Elizabeth Woodville – with no divorce that meant the Princes in the Tower were illegitimate and so the drama of Richard III took place! Joan is now the keeper of the Neolithic tombs in Addington.

Joan Scott

Joan was born in 1927 and has lived in Addington since she was two years old. She attended Addington School, can remember the shops by the village green, a doodlebug landing during the war and many changes that have taken place in the village. She was a church warden for many years, served on a number of committees and organised the Addington annual party for senior citizens with Audrey Reeves for many years.

John Cook

John was born in Blacklands, East Malling and attended the village Primary School. He has lived and worked in the village all his life.

John Easton

John Easton was born in 1940 in Ryarsh. He spent most of his working life at the East Malling Research Station, East Malling, where he became an expert in pruning and propagation. John retired in 2000 but continues to look after the fruit gardens at Bradbourne House, that are currently being revitalised, and also instructs on short practical course on pruning and grafting. He now lives in Maidstone with his family.

John Lander

John was born in Worthing, Sussex and moved to Offham in 1955 to take up the post of General Manager - Kent Hop, Fruit and Stock Farms Limited based at Aldon Farm. He later worked for the Hops Marketing Board at Paddock Wood. John was heavily involved in village life for many years and was MC for the Offham May Day event for a number of years during the sixties and seventies. He now lives in West Malling.

Kevin Wagstaff

Kevin has lived in Leybourne since 1988 and has been an active member of the community since that time. He was school governor of Leybourne Primary School for twenty years, manager of one of the youth football teams, church warden and is presently a parish councillor.

Leslie Fox

Leslie Fox has lived in East Malling for 80 years. His father's family were from East Malling and his mother was originally from Maidstone. He was born in Maidstone in June 1918, during the Great War. Leslie went to East Malling Primary School. He worked in a joiner's yard in West Malling before and after serving in World War II, during which time he was based in London. Leslie spent much of his time outside of work caring for his parents – his mother lived to be 103!

Louis Fissenden

Louis was born in Wrotham and lived there for 32 years before moving to Addington. His family have lived in the area since 1902. Two of Lou's uncles, Harry and Sydney, are commemorated on the WW1 Memorial outside St. Margaret's Church and his aunt, Gertrude Fissenden, as one of the oldest members of the community, planted the Coronation Tree in the churchyard, as a plaque beneath it records. Louis was actively involved in the Trottiscliffe Cricket Club for many years and he continues to maintain close links with the village.

Louise Parfitt

Louise was born in Ryarsh in 1967. She has a long family history in the area and has spent most of her life in Birling and Ryarsh. She attended Ryarsh Primary School, as did her children, and she now works at the school. Louise got involved with All Saints Church in Birling from a young age. She was a member of the youth group 'The Campaigners', attended the recasting of the church bells in

1986 and has even abseiled from the top of the church to raise funds. Louise was married in Birling Church in 1989 and now lives with her family in Leybourne.

Malcolm Wickenden

Malcolm Wicken-den, born 1943, moved from Maidstone to East Malling in 1960, when he started work at the East Malling Research Station. He became the Station Met Observer at the research centre for over thirty years. Malcolm moved to West Malling in 1975 where he was parish councillor and tree warden. Malcolm is now retired but is a keen walker and has been involved in 'Macey's Meadow' from the early stages of its development.

Margaret Castle

Margaret moved to Addington in the 1950s. She was originally from London but soon got involved in village life. Her husband was a cricketer and was heavily involved in the development of the cricket field and club and Margaret was a founder member of the drama club in the village.

Margaret C. Gadd (Nee West)

Margaret was born in May 1947 at Brindle Cottage, Clare Lane, East Malling. She attended school locally, worked at Chiesmans Department Store for some time and then worked for Kent County Council, in County Hall, Maidstone. Margaret was involved with the Malling Society, the local Conservative Party and the British Legion and planned several floats for the annual carnivals in West Malling. She also helped in "Foxed and Bound" – a second hand and antiquarian book shop in West Street, West Malling (now an herbalist). Margaret ran ghost tours in West Malling for several years and produced a leaflet/book on the subject. She now lives in Portland, Dorset, where she moved in 2002.

Mrs M A West

Mrs West was born in 1924 and moved to East Malling with her parents in 1939. She later moved to West Malling where, for some time, she worked for Malling Rural District Council. Mrs West was greatly involved in the West Malling Carnivals through her work with the British Legion. She now lives in Portland where she moved in 2001.

Margaret Robinson

Margaret lived in West Malling for twenty five years. She has worked as parish clerk and tree warden in the town and has been involved in several local projects - such as the WI and running crafts sessions for the Guides. Margaret was one of the original volunteers involved with the development of 'Macey's Meadow' – a community orchard project in West Malling. Margaret still volunteers for the project and has also helped to develop the parish walk. She now lives in Wateringbury but continues to maintain her links with West Malling.

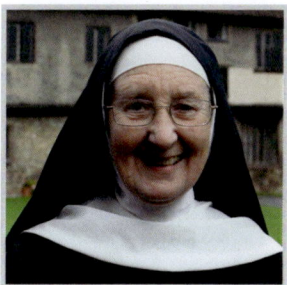

Sister Mary Mark Brooksbank OSB

Sister Mary Mark first visited St. Mary's Abbey, West Malling in 1955, when she stayed for a retreat. She returned in 1958, aged twenty three, to join the Anglican Benedictine community of nuns, having finished her nurses training. Sister Mary Mark made her vows in 1962 and has been at The Abbey ever since.

Mary Warren

Mary was born in December 1923 and lives in Larkfield. Together with her husband, she joined the Choir at Holy Trinity Church in 1961. They made many friends through the church and often helped out at jumble sales, autumn fairs & summer fetes. Mary also helped as a volunteer at St Martins (where she now lives) when it was run by the Council and supported other local elderly residents at the bingo club, and through the Methodist Church. Mary had been 'in service' since the age of 14. She later took on work cleaning houses and fruit picking. Mary recalls that the pay was low though both jobs allowed her to take her children with her.

Michael Fuller

Michael Fuller was born in October 1940, and still lives, with his wife Gloria, in his childhood home in Lunsford Lane, Larkfield. His education started at Leybourne C of E Primary School, and was completed at Maidstone Grammar School. His entire working life was spent in the paper industry, starting with A E Reed & Co at Aylesford Paper Mills. From there he moved to Barcham Green Ltd at Hayle mill, Loose, before transferring to W & R Balston Ltd at Springfield mill in Maidstone. He is a keen local historian, with a particular interest in watermills and the paper industry. His father, Leslie, was born in 1914, and married his wife, Thirza, in 1938, before setting up home in Lunsford Lane. He, also, spent his entire working life in the paper trade. He retired in 1979 as Group Analyst for the Reed Paper Group, having started with A E Reed & Co at Aylesford Paper Mills in about 1930. His paternal grandfather, Frederick, spent 55 years in the gas industry, 32 years of which were with the Mid Kent Gas Light & Coke Co at Snodland, and from which he retired in the position of Superintendent. He, too, lived in Lunsford Lane, with his wife Mildred, very close to Leslie and Thirza. Michael's maternal grandfather, Edward Gosse, was a saddler and harness maker, who followed his trade at his shop in King Street, Maidstone.

Mike Towler

Mike, born in 1932, has lived in Trottiscliffe for thirty seven years. He was an engineer and therefore, took responsibility for the 'Trosley Towers Bridge' project leading up to the acquisition of the bridge by the Trottiscliffe Society in 1996, and the subsequent restoration work. Mike was a founder member of The Trottiscliffe Society and also helped to restore the Wetlands – the last of a series of medieval ponds. Mike is an avid enthusiast of British Wildlife and has a particularly keen interest in, and great knowledge of, badgers and foxes. He has 'befriended' many wild foxes, as well as looking after other foxes through his connections with fox rescue projects.

Dr Richard Morrice

Richard is an architectural historian & author, and sometime English Heritage Inspector for Kent. He attended Mereworth School when his father was stationed at West Malling.

Ron Martin

Ron Martin was born in Wateringbury in 1938 and moved to West Malling aged one. He attended Leybourne Primary and West Malling Primary, before going on to Malling Boys School until age 11. He then attended Maidstone Grammar School. His first job was at Fremlins before he went off to join the RAF. Ron returned to West Malling later and became very involved with the football in the town, as well as in the fundraising for the village hall. In 1975 he moved to Snodland. Ron is an active member of the Malling Society and has written three books on the history of pubs in the area. Ron also is producing a series of books recording the memories of local residents in the early 20th century, has researched and put together several exhibitions on local history for The Malling Society and is currently researching the 1914 – 1918 war, in readiness for the next exhibition in 2014.

Roy Keeler

Roy comes from a traditional Kent woodland family and was born in East Kent before moving to Mereworth in 1953, when his father took the position of Woodreeve at the Mereworth Estate. Roy took over the position of 'Woodreeve' after his father – a role his son has subsequently filled when Roy retired five years ago. Roy's other son is also involved in the wood business, as a tree surveyor.

Roy has a keen interest in cricket and is Chair of Mereworth Cricket Club.

Stephen Betts

Stephen is the fourth generation of the Betts family to be running Laurence J Betts Ltd, founded in 1901 and based at Church Farm, Offham. Stephen was brought up on the farm and attended Leybourne Primary School before going to boarding school when he was older. In 1980, he went to Uganda to set up a farming project for TEAR Fund and when he returned in 1982, he became manager of the farm. His brother, Ian also works on the farm having joined the business in 1987. Stephen is Churchwarden at St Michael's Church, Offham.

Stuart Millson (born 27 June 1965).

Stuart has lived in the East Malling area since 1998, although he first came to the village in 1987. He is the one, independent, Councillor (elected in 2007) on East Malling and Larkfield Parish Council, and serves on two committees: Planning and Allotments and Open Spaces. Planning and conservation are subjects about which he is passionate, and prompted his involvement in local politics. Stuart is also the Chairman of the local branch of The Royal Society of St. George – the Society, nationally, was founded in 1894. The Branch helps to raise money for local charities and other good causes, and played an active role in the village's 2012 Jubilee celebrations.

Stuart Olsson

Stuart was born in Enfield in 1941. He first encountered the Women's land Army when he was five years old and has been captivated by their story ever since. Stuart campaigned for a badge of honour of the Women's Land Army and was successful in achieving this in 2007. He joined the Ministry of Agriculture in 1968 and followed a long career there. Stuart lives in Larkfield, where he has played an active part in the community for many years. He is Area Coordinator for Neighbourhood Watch, Larkfield, and Chair of the North Larkfield Group for the Protection of the Environment that recently ran a successful campaign to clean up St Martin's Square, Larkfield.

Sydney (Syd) Gilliard and Josephine (Jo) Crittall

Syd and Jo are brother and sister whose family lived in Offham many years ago. After retirement in February 2011, Jo rekindled her interest in researching the Gilliard family history. Of particular interest was the research of a family story, about a shooting incident where their great aunt (Winifred) was shot, and died, aged 8 years, on 21 June 1897. Jo and Syd came along to the Offham Community Heritage Workshop to see if they could find out more about the incident, and if they could discover the whereabouts of the police house, in Offham, at the time of the incident... Syd now lives in Aylesford and Jo lives in Birling.

CONTRIBUTORS AND THEIR STORIES

Sylvia Butler

Sylvia was born in August 1939 at her grandfather's house in Addington. Her grandfather, Alfred C Chapman, had been the Farm Bailiff. Her mother had attended Addington School until she went into service aged 14, where she progressed to be head cook. Sylvia was christened, confirmed and married in Addington Church, as was her mother before her - her daughter followed the family tradition and was christened and married there too! Sylvia, and her brother, attended Addington School where Sylvia can recall the unpleasant experience of having to line up each morning and being forced to take a spoonful of cod liver oil or malt! When Addington School closed they went to Ryarsh School. After Sylvia married, she travelled the world with her husband Brian and her two children (Brian was in the REME) before returning to live at her childhood home in Ryarsh in 1972.

Significant People and Visitors – *Community,* *Church* *and a Royal Visitor, Addington*

Tim Baldock

Tim's family have been involved in West Malling life for several generations. They have owned and run independent shops in the town, and fully embraced local life by supporting, and getting involved in, all the village and royal events of the day. Tim has been involved in the Chamber of Commerce, the West Malling Carnivals, the Malling Society and was Scout Master for many years.

Historical Buildings and Sites of Interest - *Tunnels* *West Malling*
Village Life - *Rock and Roll at the Airfield*

Tony Briggs

Tony Briggs was born in March 1935 and has a long family history in the area. His grandfather, Arthur Thomas, first took over the bakery premises in West Malling in 1888. Tony attended the Malling Boys School and remembers the impact that the war had on West Malling, and how the subsequent rationing affected local people and the family business. He helped in the bakehouse as a young man, then took over the family business in 1963. As his father had declared the bakery business bankrupt in the 1950s, Tony ran the shop as a general store until 1988. He still lives with his wife, June, next door to his shop in the High Street, West Malling.

Local Businesses and Employment - *'A Briggs'* *Bakery West Malling*

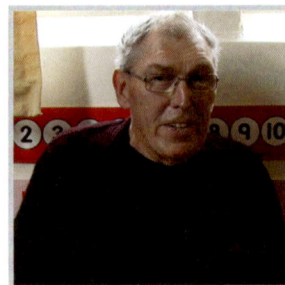

Trevor Lingham

Trevor was born in January 1949 at Paddlesworth Farm. He grew up on the farm and has had a lifelong connection with Birling, having spent much of his youth in the village playing with his best friend and attending Birling Youth Club. His wife, Denise, was from Snodland but also had childhood connections with Birling and they lived there together for a few years in the early 1980s, before moving to Paddlesworth with their three daughters in 1986.

Trudy Dean

Trudy Dean moved to West Malling over thirty years ago. She made a point of getting to know about West Malling, and the people of the town, through taking on the role of bookings secretary of the village hall. She then worked as Parish Clerk, before getting more directly involved in local politics through the Parish Council and, from 1985, the County Council.

Trudy is currently County Councillor for Malling Central. She is also Chairman of West Malling Parish Council, Chairman of the Malling Action Partnership (MAP) and Leader of the Kent County Council Lib Dem Group. Trudy has a keen interest in the environment and is a staunch supporter of all things 'Malling'.

Valerie Valvassura

Valerie was born in 1945 and raised in the Malling area. She has been actively involved in local life for many years, as a Parish Councillor and through a range of voluntary work. She worked for Kent County Council, coordinating transport for schools, and is now retired. Valerie lives in the house she bought with her husband in 1966 on London Road, Leybourne.

Wendy King

Wendy moved to East Malling with her family in 1954. She went to the school at Manningham House and attended the Church Choir and Church Youth Club. Her first job was as a typist at East Malling Research Station before working as a secretary for various solicitors in Maidstone. She also worked for Barclays Bank in Larkfield and Maidstone, before deciding on a change in 1983, when she went to work for the Royal Mail. Wendy stayed with the Royal Mail for twenty nine years, retiring at the end of 2011.

2 3

STORIES BY SUBJECT

STORIES BY SUBJECT

AGRICULTURE

Church Farm, 1932

Church Farm, Offham

Stephen Betts

On returning to Church farm after the First World War, my Grandfather, Laurence J Betts, continued farming hops until their decline in 1930, where-upon he started growing vegetables on the 60 acres of land.

Through those early years of vegetables, my Grandfather also introduced livestock to the farm. He developed a pedigree dairy herd of Ayrshire cows and a prize winning pedigree herd of Romney Sheep. Over the following years, a large number of these sheep were exported to New Zealand and Argentina for breeding, as they were a highly sought after stock of the famous Kent Breed.

My father, Stewart Betts, started working on the farm in 1949. He introduced pigs into the farm and developed a good name for pedigree Large White boars and gilts, which were sold for breeding - so we were a mixed farm with vegetables, potatoes, cereals, pigs, sheep and dairy, all the way through until 1978, when I came back to the farm to look after the pigs, having been at The Royal Agricultural College, Cirencester.

By this time my grandfather had retired and, following my return from Uganda in 1982,

I helped my father run the farm and I've been running the farm pretty much ever since, with the aid of my brother Ian.

Now, our father's also retired, and we're just looking toward the next generation to, hopefully, come along and help us take the business forward...

We currently specialise in growing cereals and salads - lettuce and leafy salads. We discontinued the sheep, the pigs and the dairy and now, more recently, we have stopped growing potatoes and most of the vegetables - as customer demand changes.

Sheep at Church Farm, 1956

27

Basically, now it's cereals and lettuce, which sounds like just two crops but, in actual fact, we grow more than 17 different types of lettuce and leafy salads and employ 110 people - so it's still a challenging job.

Church Farm, Offham had been in the same family for 355 years before it was put up for sale by Lord Hothfield, in May 1901. The farm was bought by Colonel Sofer Whitburn of Addington and J.R Betts became the tenant later that year.
J.R Betts and his predecessors had farmed at Otham near Maidstone since the 16th century. His son, Laurence J Betts, helped his father to run the farms and eventually, when Church Farm, Offham came up for sale in 1923, he bought the farm together with an uncle and W. Sharp. The three went on to form Laurence J. Betts Ltd. in 1930.
All the hops were grubbed out and vegetables, potatoes, lettuce and many other crops were grown.
In 1933 a new house was built opposite Offham Primary School and Laurence J. Betts moved in with his wife and family.
Over the years, the farm has grown in size as extra land has been bought. In 1966, part of Fatherwell Farm was purchased from Mr Hitch. The neighbouring Godwell Farm was rented in 1977 and purchased in 1981.
The farm now farms over 1300 acres and supplies processors who produce bags of salad leaves for supermarkets, and also several large wholesalers in Kent and Sussex who supply hospitals, schools, restaurants, pubs and other big users. The company has a policy of investing in the very latest technology to remain at the forefront of crop production.

Fruit and Orchards, West Malling
Molly Potts

When I moved here it was all soft fruits for the canning over at Yalding, where the Smedley Factory was... and there used to be gooseberries and strawberries and raspberries. And there were the orchards... we used to pick the apples for cider making...

Once the canning industry moved and the common market sort of took over, I think a lot of farmers were doing 'pick your own' strawberries and fruit. And they couldn't get rid of the apples because of foreign imports. So yeah! It's changed a lot!

Smedleys in Yalding closed in the early 1970s.

Hop Picking, Offham
John Lander

Well, in those days, hop farming was very different from what it is today. A lot of the work was manual. Hops, in those days, were grown on high wire work, which had to be strung - and that was all done by hand. And then, of course, all the picking was by hand - where it's all done these days by machine.

At the onset of hop picking, we used to send postcards to all the people who came down from London to advise them of the day for the start of hop picking - and they would come down by train or car and they lived on the farm during the period of hop picking, in huts which were fairly primitive. But it occurred during the month of September, so the weather, normally, was fairly kind to them during that month. Normally, hop picking only lasted for a month. Sometimes, it went into the first week of October, depending on the size of the crop and so forth. And it was all piece work and the hop pickers picked into open bins...

Pickers could get a sub during the course of

Hop Picking at Aldon Farm, 1912

hop picking - but the final payment was not made to them until the end of hop picking - and that was quite a big operation in itself, because all the hop picking books had to be tallied up overnight. We had to rush to the bank in the morning to get the money, which was quite considerable - and then they were all paid off and they went back to London.

They came mostly from the East End of London. There were a few rogues amongst them but, on the whole, they were a jolly lot of people. They worked very hard, most of them, and they were pretty well law-abiding.

The village of Offham would always get a bit panicky about their arrival because they thought all sorts of dreadful things would happen to them. The shop and post office used to cover its counter with wire netting to prevent pilfering – but, on the whole, I think they were fairly honest. They used to nick a bit of fruit but not disastrously so. I think the publicans used to make a charge for the glasses so that they made sure they got them back when they were finished drinking ...but it was a relatively trouble-free time – and, of course, the number of pickers on Aldon farm practically doubled the population of the village when they were in residence - so it was a very big influx of people into a small community.

I should have mentioned that, as well as the pickers that came down from London, there were local hop pickers from the village - and the school holidays were extended through the end of September in those days, to enable the school children to accompany their parents. The older ones would probably do a bit of picking and earn some pocket money.

Spiders Hall Farm, Leybourne
Bob Clarke

Right behind where the bypass and motorway goes... well that used to be Spiders Hall Farm, partly... And it used to belong to a little old lady and her sister Miss Johnson and her sister Daisy... And anybody who stepped over her fence... all of a sudden this little apparition used to appear, about 5ft tall, wearing a black beret, black dress and sack tied round her middle! So nobody ever tried anything ... You had to keep to the footpath!

The Fruit Pickers of Mereworth
Alison Lowe and her daughter Marion Regan

Alison   The ladies from the estates used to come out with their children. We had crèches for the babies...

Marion   We used to run double decker buses from the sixties... to Larkfield, Snodland and Tonbridge.

Alison   They loved coming out and getting a tan... Earning money for their holidays and getting a tan in their bikinis as they were picking the fruit. There were a lot of people with rather bad sunburn in those days!

Marion   I think what's interesting about who picked the fruit is that when you (mum) first came to the village, it would have been local ladies who picked the strawberries and also apples. And then in the 1970's, a large number of Vietnamese people were settled on the Airfield Estate, when it was still council owned, and they were basically economic refugees... quite a few of them came and picked fruit.
Before then, we had some Ugandan Asians who were also settled up there and they used to come and pick fruit.
And then for a period in the seventies, probably fifty percent of our strawberry pickers were

Vietnamese, and there will be people in the village who remember that period. And it probably only lasted about four or five years, because then they all moved into the bigger economy and started coming back and visiting us in bigger and bigger cars... and their children went off to university and they became doctors and dentists and teachers - which is what they probably were back home, when they first arrived. But it gave them their first rung into this economy.

And now of course we don't have any Vietnamese people picking fruit, but we did for a period with their conical hats - cooking up great things on the headland for lunch!

Then, after that group of people, the local ladies with children... it no longer became an attractive job for them. Because firstly, they'd moved into full-time employment, so they didn't just want a few weeks' work in the summer. But more importantly, we couldn't have children on the farm because of the Children's Act (1989). It was just very difficult - you had to have fully qualified people to look after the children on the headland. You used to just select one of the mums to look after the other children. You couldn't do that anymore...

And so then we were really saved by the coming down of the Berlin Wall (1989) because that freed up a large number of Eastern European, former Soviet countries, and their young people wanted to come and pick fruit. And they came on a scheme which was licensed by the Home Office to come and pick fruit for a few months each year. And we still have quite a lot of those people who came on that scheme - their family members or they themselves, because those countries have (now) joined the EU, and they come and they stay on the farm, and they're the majority of the people who pick fruit now.

Barons Place is an old-established and important farm in Mereworth, owned in the 17th and 18th centuries by the Vanes, Lords Barnard and Viscounts Vane. By 1840 it was owned by the 7th Viscount Torrington and occupied by the Langridge family as farming tenants growing fruit and hops. In 1893 Bernard Champion rented Barons Place farm and, as Champion Bros., grew fruit with his elder brother Horace. He bought the farm before the Great War and it passed eventually to his grandson Hugh Lowe, who expanded it considerably. His daughter, Marion Regan, is now a major soft fruit grower.

Women's Land Army and Timber Corps
Stuart Olsson

Food was becoming very short as all the men had got up and left the farms, so it was important that the cows were milked, the animals were fed, the pigs were fed, the cabbages were grown and there was still meat production. So the women were doing the job on the farms that the men had left - to go and fight in the war. They had actually replaced them, and the country owes them a tremendous debt for what they did. Particularly my generation, because we may not have been here had the food not been produced.

Some ladies actually carried on working on the farms after the war. There really were some fantastic ladies about. Not all of them gave up, because the Women's Land Army stayed in operation until 1950, whereas the Timber Corps actually officially stopped in 1946 - though many of the girls just carried on working in the forests. So there was a real interest in the jobs they did. I don't know how many, but there were quite a number who married farmers after the war.

One of the reasons they needed the Timber Corps was because the Bevan boys were working in the mines in Wales and they hadn't got the pit props to prop the mines up. So they needed the timber. That was the original job the girls did - they actually went out and got the pit props for the boys.

Then the Navy needed repairs to ships, then there was the mosquito which was eighty per cent wood - so there was wood needed for aircraft. The Timber Corps did a tremendous job and in the process, many of them were killed by trees falling.

> The new badge that Stuart campaigned for, instituted in 2007, signifies the Government's recognition of the work that the Women's Land Army contributed during the war.

Women's Land Army and Timber Corps badge

Mereworth Woods

Roy Keeler

It's not understood these days the amount of work that the woodland supplied. I can remember, even in my early days, when we used to hold the wood sale day down at the 'Queen's Head'. There would be twenty or thirty chaps inside buying cants of wood, but there would be as many outside looking for jobs as woodcutters.

We would have probably thirty odd chaps back then, working either for themselves or for bigger wood-buying companies, working within the Wood. They would be busy making up the wood that they cut during the winter, and that would take them right through the summer.

Some of them used to, in fact, leave off for a period in the Spring when the cherries were about - buy a bit of cherries and make money at that.

They'd finish their wood... They generally tried to get that finished in time for the hop picking and the fruit picking season. Then,

we'd be back to the last Monday in October when the last of the apples was finished and then that would be wood sale time... they'd be back into the Wood again, and they'd work the Wood right through.

> Mereworth Woods are very ancient and form part of the dense timber covering of the greensand ridge. They have been grown for centuries for coppice for making charcoal, fencing and construction materials. In the middle ages they formed part of the estate of the great Nevill family whose descendants still own a large part of them.

CHURCH

Acts of Kindness

Sister Mary Mark

W. Orme, our butcher, is a small family firm, and 50 years ago they had their own farm and livestock. I believe they did their own slaughtering too. One day, in the mid 1980's, the old Mr Orme delivered the meat to the guest house kitchen where I was working. On his way out he noticed a large bowl of 'mash' that was cooling outside the back door with a label on it saying 'THIS IS NOT COMPOST BUT FOR THE BIRDIES'. Turning back, he asked if I was feeding the birds - it was January and we were deep in snow – later that day I found a parcel of several pounds of raw suet that he had returned with for the birds! I thought that was so kind!

Our local roofers, a small firm run by John Large, are kindness itself. There was one year, when they were retiling the guest house roof during January, when the guest house was closed. They had almost finished when dry rot was discovered in the porch timbers and it all had to be stripped and rebuilt. The guest house was due to reopen in a week or so and the porch entrance hall had to be useable. The weather was appalling, bitterly cold and frosty, or wet with rain or snow. John and his team put themselves out to get the work finished, normally they wouldn't have worked in that weather. John was heard to remark, when they finished, "We would only have done that for the Abbey".

A few years ago, we found that somebody was leaving us gifts of grapes at the gate. A few weeks later, the Infirmarian* was waiting for a prescription at the chemists when a booming voice said "Did you like the grapes sister?" Somewhat surprised and embarrassed the Sister replied, "Yes, yes, thank you, we enjoyed them". The gentleman then went on… "I says to my Nell, 'I bet them nuns don't get much in the way of fruit except apples and rhubarb, so I'll give 'em a treat' ". He kindly treated us to several boxes of grapes that year. Alas, we never discovered who he was.

More recently, Andy Graham had a greengrocer's store in the arcade where we bought our fruit and vegetables. He tried to sell as much local grown produce as he could

obtain. Quite often at the end of the week he would send us a box of vegetables and fruit that he knew would not keep fresh over the weekend. (Sadly, he couldn't compete with Tesco's and has had to move elsewhere.)

*An Infirmarian is a person having charge of an infirmary, especially in a monastic institution.

Holy Trinity Church, New Hythe Lane

Mary Warren and Derek Brown

Mary My husband was churchwarden for forty years at Holy Trinity, New Hythe Lane, and we both joined the choir. We had a lovely social life through the church. My son was 15 months when we came to Larkfield. They used to say, "Bring him along in his pram and put him at the end of the church." Trouble was he used to make noises - but they didn't worry… There was always something to do - flower arranging, harvest time, decorating the church… We had a family service and mothers brought their children along so the church got packed. Derek came to the same church as I did…

Derek The church in Larkfield has changed its name twice in my memory. It started off being built as a daughter church of East Malling. After the war, it became a parish in its own right with its own vicar. Then, they

Holy Trinity Church, Larkfield

came to the conclusion that with the development going on, the centre of the parish was no longer within the church - it was on the fringe, so they changed it from Holy Trinity, New Hythe, to Holy Trinity, Larkfield - and that change came about in 1961, I think.

Holy Trinity Church, Larkfield, was built by the Wigan family of Clare House in about 1853. It was designed by R.P. Poipe and has an interesting 'wheel window' feature at the western end. From 1854 it was a chapel of ease to St James, East Malling. It became a separate church parish in 1949 as New Hythe Church - and then later, when Larkfield had grown, it was renamed Larkfield Church. Its first curate was Nathaniel Dimmock who had married one of the Wigan family daughters.

Leybourne Church
Kevin Wagstaff

When Father Jeffrey moved on, the attendance at church was really blossoming. We'd got a really active church choir, we'd got an active youth group, an active Sunday Club, and we appointed our own Priest in Charge.

The two church wardens at the time, Steven Thomas and Roy Guest, asked me to go up to Crayford to watch this priest at one of his services, so I snuck in at the back and watched this service. This was at an 8 'o clock service, and the priest was Father Chris Dench. And then I came back down here at 10 'o clock to report back my observations, and there at the back of the church was Father Chris Dench doing a similar thing down here to see what he thought of the Parish. And I guess the rest is sort of history, as they say.

We appointed Father Chris as Parish Priest - that would have been about 1995. And we also made a case to the then Bishop of Rochester, that Father Chris should be actually

appointed as Vicar of Leybourne. We were able to demonstrate that we could financially support our own Vicar and the Bishop agreed with that, and so, for the first time in about thirty or forty years - Leybourne had its own Vicar.

Leybourne Church, 1997.

Leybourne Church originally dates back to Saxon times though it has been changed significantly over the years. When originally built it had three bells but when the tower collapsed in 1580, only two bells were restored. The tower was changed again in 1874 when architect Sir Arthur Blomfeld encased it in an extra layer of wall. On 10 June 1966, the tower was hit by a bolt of lightning and caught fire. Many parish records were destroyed by the fire. It was subsequently decided to only have one bell.
Leybourne Church has very strong connections with Leybourne Castle, the seat of the de Leybourne family, who had originally come over with William the Conqueror.
Sir Roger de Leybourne accompanied Prince Edward (later Edward I) on a crusade to the Holy Land in 1270. He became ill and died during the journey and, as was his wish, his heart was embalmed, put in a lead casket and sent back to Leybourne. His heart remains in St George's Chapel at Leybourne Church and is known as the 'Heart Shrine'.

CHURCH

Ryarsh Church

Brenda Botteril

I have seen nine vicars here and a Reverend Lawson baptised me, and I've still got my baptism certificate. When I joined the choir, we had to wear a white gown with a veil across our head, and when, in 1962, there was a Reverend Noel Bone came here, he didn't like us as he called, 'nurses', so we changed over to red cassocks and a white surplice, and we are still wearing those now. Mine has a rough edge to it, because I've been in the choir longer than anyone else, and it's worn out! But, it should see my lifetime out... hopefully!

Reverend Bone and Cyril Botteril putting the new weather vane on Ryarsh Church, 1968

Brenda has given over seventy years' service to the music at Ryarsh Church. St. Martin's, a 12th century foundation, stands at a little distance to the main village, which shifted its focus many centuries ago, possibly after the Black Death. By 1237 it was in the possession of the Priory of Merton, Surrey. As such it was served by a Vicar and was dedicated to St. Lawrence. The dedication changed to St. Martin because his saint's day was in June, rather than at harvest-time! The Advowson later came into the hands of the Watton family of Addington, whose descendants held it until the 20th century.

In common with many other small parishes, Ryarsh combined (with Birling) during the mid 20th century. In 1975, following the death of Rev. John MacDonald, Rector of Addington and Trottiscliffe, the Vicar of Ryarsh, Rev. Malcolm Bury, was asked to serve as priest in charge for these two parishes as well. This arrangement is now permanent and is known as the United Benefice of Birling, Addington, Ryarsh and Trottiscliffe, or BART for short. The present Rector is Rev. Dr. Linda Shuker, who lives in the Vicarage opposite Ryarsh School.

The Abbey 900th Anniversary, West Malling

Sister Mary Mark

In 1990 we kept our 900th anniversary of the founding of the Abbey and the village took this up in the most wonderful way...

The Tonbridge and Malling Council produced a commemoration brochure and they printed 5,000 copies. They asked the Archbishop of Canterbury, the Bishop of Rochester, and various people to write appreciations of the Abbey and listed all the celebration events that were to take place. They appointed a committee with one or two of the Sisters to work on it.

They were very keen to have an exhibition of our life and work and the historic buildings. We provided photographs and scripted headings and wrote some of the texts. This exhibition travelled widely to the Cathedral, schools, churches and other institutions between May

St. Mary's Abbey, 12th century Norman Tower and Guesthouse

and October. The Parish magazine had pen and ink drawings of the Abbey drawn by two of our Sisters as its cover illustration that year.

Then the various events that we shared with the community…

The school children produced a play of 'George and the Dragon' that starred Bishop Gundulf. They came to the Abbey on June 20th to give us a performance, and did so on the lawn in front of the tower and it was delightful.

We held open days for the village in June and early July. The Sisters arranged guided tours of the ancient buildings and the church and cloisters. There would be several groups waiting for the tours and they still do this when we have the Heritage Days in September.

On July 1st we had a shared parish Eucharist and the congregation from St. Mary's came to us for the service. They processed down the High Street from the church and in through the big gates and came into our church… That was really lovely - the church was packed!

View from East Malling Church
Stuart Millson

One of the most interesting recollections that I have is of the old days when Leslie Rogers was the church warden, and one day back in about 1996, Mr. Rogers allowed me to go to the very top of the church tower, as I was keen to see the view.

It was a beautiful early summer's day and I turned 360 degrees, surveying the scene at all points of the compass. I really appreciated the profound sense of East Malling being a community - a real village still - protected by the playing fields, the Research Station land and the orchards and we are blessed by a beautiful array of trees. So there's a strong sense of greenery and cohesion and that sense was made apparent to me on that day by Leslie Rogers.

Malling Abbey was founded as a Benedictine nunnery c. 1090 by Bishop Gundulf of Rochester, who guided the nuns until his death in 1108. Avice, who had served as Gundulf's prioress, was then appointed as the first abbess by Gundulf on his death-bed. The Abbey survived with mixed fortunes until it was dissolved in 1538, and then remained in private ownership until 1892, when it was purchased by Charlotte Boyd and given to the Sisterhood of SS Mary and Scholastica, Twickenham. Faced with numerous difficulties, the Sisterhood left Malling in 1911, and, following several years of negotiations, the present community of Anglican Benedictine nuns moved from Baltonsborough near Glastonbury to West Malling in 1916.

COMMUNITY PROJECTS AND AMENITIES DEVELOPMENT

Addington Village Hall

David Cameron

I'd been to a function at the old Village Hall (down behind 'The Angel') which was an old First World War hut... and there were no proper amenities - only space for four cars for parking, so it caused a lot of aggravation from the pub owner.

Anyway, I said, "Why can't we build a hall on the Recreation Ground?" ... and the committee didn't agree with me, because they'd been on the committee a long time and I was new to the place so new ideas didn't go down very well.

But anyway, in the end we called a public meeting and about 50 people attended - and it's quoted in the Kent Messenger... and they accepted my idea.

My idea was to sell the plot where the old one was, raise some money locally to build this (new) Village Hall.

I went down to Bethersden - a firm called 'Colts' where they specialised in building this type of building... Set sizes... so they were already drawn up - it was all ready to go to a local authority and for £28,000 they built it... and it's been fantastic ever since - all that time.

Up until the First World War, Addington village just had a 'Club Room' beside the Angel public house, where the Men's Club met and other functions took place. At one time it housed a small donated library. The owner of the manor, Col. Sofer-Whitburn, also owned the freehold of most of the centre of the village He had commanded the Royal West Kent Yeomanry from 1914-1921 and, before he sold his entire Kent estate in 1924, he donated a small plot of land on Millhouse Lane for the parish to site a village hall. This was his farewell present to the village. He also gave a redundant army hut to use for this purpose. The hall was much used for 40 years, even though it did not boast electricity until the 1940's and had insufficient parking facilities. Addington Amateur Dramatic Society staged a number of well received productions there, and it was partly their needs that spurred the village to build a new hall next to a small cricket pavilion on the Recreation Ground. The Hall still serves the village well, and has, over the years, upgraded its facilities to meet changing needs.

Cricket and Drama in Addington

Margaret Castle

I am a trained teacher and after my sons, Ian and Glen, were established at school, I managed to get a teaching job, which I thoroughly enjoyed. And then I decided I needed something to stretch me a bit further, so I took a LAMDA* teaching certificate - so I became a drama teacher, as well. And that also initiated other things...

My husband was an interested cricketer and got together with some pals in the village pub, 'The Angel', and they decided it was about time they had a cricket team.

*LAMDA stands for The London Academy of Music and Dramatic Art.

At that time, Richard Boyle had a piece of land and he offered it to the village club, (well the people that had got together then) - for nothing. And the parish council said, "Well you can't do that, you know, we've got to have something legal", so they sorted it out between them. The land that is now Addington Village Cricket Club initiated... our first pavilion was a marquee.

We didn't have any water laid on, they didn't have any dressing rooms, but a hessian curtain across the marquee, and they had to change their clothes behind the hessian, with hooks for them to hang things on... and there were trestle tables that all folded down and stored in 'Rose Alba'. And the water came from Rose Alba as well... in dust bins. They filled the clean dust bins, new clean dust bins - they filled them up with water and trailed them over there! Other arrangements were very, rural! But we had a wonderful time! And the children also had a wonderful time!

Then later on a few of the villagers got together and they thought it was time we had a dramatic society. One of those was Peter Rimmer, who had stayed with me. His mother and father had had, at one time, the village shop. He was a reporter and was working at that time on the Sevenoaks Chronicle. He, with one or two others, decided to get together to form this dramatic society.

The village hall at that time was a little tiny, ex-Army hut, which was just down past 'The Angel', and it wasn't very big, and the stage was even smaller. When I think of the productions we put on there and the trials and tribulations we had! But what fun we had doing them. We stayed there until they said, "No, you can't do it anymore - the electrics are no good, they're dangerous, they could catch fire. You can't put on any more performances". So that was rather sad. Many of us still wanted to go on acting. So we went to Borough Green for a while and we went with the 'Borograds'. But then they built the Village Hall which was

First Match of Addington Cricket Club, 1959

'Rose Alba' is a house in the village that was built for Richard Boyle who later became Sir Richard Boyle, 4th Bart. (1930-1983).

wonderful. A person called Bill Rawson was the main instigator of that. The Village Hall was built and the stage was built and the dressing rooms and we couldn't believe it! And then we had our first production which was an Alan Ayckbourn play (Time and Time Again). We went from strength to strength after that and became a well-known group.

East Malling Conservation Group
Diz Bernal

In 1986 I was already living with my family in East Malling and we were not the only ones to be increasingly concerned about the way the village was being developed. It was resulting in two separate villages. There was the north side where several housing developments were built and the south side was the old village, so two very disparate groups of people really. And, in between, there was part of the old Clare Park estate (South Ward playing fields). So, that was the dividing line if you like.

We weren't happy with the way things were going because we felt that the village should be for everybody - not just two separate parts to it. And I remember my husband and a few other men met in the 'King and Queen' one night to see what they could do... and to plan. And when he came back home he said, "Right, yes, we've started. We're going to call ourselves the 'East Malling Conservation Group' and I put your name down for a membership!"

Things went swimmingly, once we got going. We established reasonable relations with the Borough Council. We already had good relations with the Parish Council and we were doing well until there was a hiccup and things started to go downhill. And it looked at one point as if the conservation group would have to be rolled up. There was very little money in the kitty, there seemed to be a lack of oomph about everybody.

I, by that time, was the Vice Chairman and the Chairman was often not in the country. So, I called a meeting in the village school hall and a lot of people came and, to my great relief, there was a lot of enthusiasm because of the purpose of the conservation group. Nobody who lived in the village wanted to see their village messed up with wrong planning, which was what was happening. We've gone from strength to strength since then. That was twenty five years ago... something like that. And it's doing well now - we've lost some battles, you're bound to. But we also have won some.

And so that, in essence... that's the story of East Malling Conservation Group.

> The East Malling Conservation Group is still going strong and currently has around 100 members.

LEYARA (Leybourne Active Retirement Association)

David Fillery

I don't know what started it (the formation of Active Retirement Associations). It probably began with a few people getting fed up with watching telly and wanting something more challenging and active to do. I think that was about twenty years ago. It grew rapidly and now there's something like 140 clubs in Kent.

Pat (Williamson) was instrumental in getting it started in Leybourne. My wife and I had tried to join another club in Leybourne but there was a two year waiting list so, when we saw LEYARA was going to start up, we came along.

> 'Active Retirement Associations' started in Kent about 25 years ago and formed under the group KENTARA. LEYARA started in 2011.

Macey's Meadow, West Malling

Margaret Robinson

So the Parish Council, Trudy Dean in particular, discovered it (the land) was going up for auction, so along she went... She got it...

Having got it, she then went to the Parish Council and said, "Well, we've got it. What we going to do with it?", and they decided to put in a steering committee. Well, there were about forty people at the first steering committee. There wasn't room to sit down. From those forty people, a little group of about eight of us sort of got together, and we decided that the best thing to do was to see what people wanted. So we got out a questionnaire and it was delivered to everybody in West Malling, and when I analysed it, mixed woodland was very high on it, and so was wildflower meadow. In fact, I think wildflower meadow was the highest, then mixed woodland, orchard, green space...

And we got a thirty-six thousand pound grant from DEFRA.

The first thing we did was clear the little bit by the cricket meadow, because everybody could see that, and I said, "Look. If we clear that, people will see that we're doing something and we'll leave that as a green space." So we cleared that - it probably took about six months to clear it - and we had numerous people came - we must have had sometimes as many as thirty people turn up.

And we had an opening ceremony. Alan West, who keeps the sheep over there now - he had a brilliant idea. He said, "Supposing we ask people to donate a tree in memory of a loved one, charge them ten pounds and do a roll of honour and say who it is that they're remembering?" And I think we collected two thousand pounds at the opening ceremony - which all went towards the purchase of this mixed woodland.

On the day we first started to plant the mixed woodland, I got in touch with every person that I was going to plant a tree for and said, "If you would like to come and plant your tree, you're very welcome", and crowds of people turned out, all to plant their tree very seriously and to have their photographs taken by it. It was a lovely day.

We raked in a few more people and planted the apple trees. Then we planted another orchard. And then we planted, lastly, the cherry orchard.

We've also got a nut platt*... When Liz Eddie died tragically, her son, Adam, who worked over with us, said, "I don't want flowers." He said, "I know what flowers Mum liked", and he did. He said, "I want donations for the meadow." Well, we got another two thousand pounds and Liz always wanted a nut platt so we bought the nut trees for that...

*A Nut Platt is a small area of planted Kentish Cobnut.

Macey's Meadow was named after Percy 'Mac' Macey. He was a local person who had been a parish councillor and had contributed a great deal to the local community and had died unexpectedly in March 1997. The land that Macey's Meadow now occupies was previously owned by the Hollands family. Whilst the Hollands family had grown many varieties of apples and cherries on the land since 1918, it had stood derelict for many years when it was bought by West Malling Parish Council in 1998.

The meadow, from the onset, has been managed and maintained by a group of volunteers of which Margaret is one. Malcolm Wickenden, Micky Pearce (Mick the tractor) and Alan West are the other key volunteers whose involvement and long term support of the project have made Macey's Meadow such a great success.

The Cricket Pavilion, Addington
David Cameron

The chairman of the cricket club was a chap named Jim Francis, and all his family were involved in the cricket ... nice family. And I said

to him one day, "Jim, what do you think about building a new pavilion? You've got enough skills in the village here with various people to get one built." And I said, "Look, I'll tell you what I'll do ... I'll supply all the insulation material for it". They went ahead and did it and it has been a great success. I know they've built more on ... it's more elaborate now ... made a lovely facility of it.

In 1959, the Recreation Ground was sold to the Parish Council for a very reasonable amount by Richard Boyle. The newly founded Addington Village Cricket Club members then personally levelled the sloping site, and the first fixture took place in 1960, with a marquee as the first pavilion. The second pavilion was a redundant holiday home donated to the Club by Lord Plunket, of The Mount (see below under, "A Royal Visitor, Addington"). This was in use until the mid 1970's when the members themselves built a permanent pavilion with their own labour. It was opened in 1979. Since then, as David tells us above, it has been extended and improved and the Cricket Club has gone from strength to strength.

The Offham Society
Mike Rowe

The Offham society was formed in 1978 and it was formed really on the back of the threat to an ancient building in the village - 'Comp Farmhouse', which was about to be demolished. Frank Johns who was a great friend of mine, who suddenly died a few years ago - he was a tax inspector by profession, but a very well qualified amateur historian, he got together a group of people in the village to fight the demolition of this 'Comp Farmhouse'... which was successfully preserved and is now a residence, and on the back of that, formed the 'Offham Society', which is a local amenity society whose objectives are the protection of the village and development of it and also to encourage sociability in the village and mount lectures and have different events during the year... and it's been going ever since.

Comp Farmhouse.

Trottiscliffe Tennis Courts

Ann Kemp

The land to the south of the village, the agricultural land, was up for sale. There was a lot of concern about what was going to happen... were people going to build thousands of houses on it and everything else? And I was in the happy position of being able to buy it.

At the same time, it had been mooted that tennis courts in the village would be something worthwhile. So, I was happy to be able to donate the small corner of a field next to the village hall for the tennis courts and a bit further down where the old pond was, now called

The tennis courts were installed c. 1990, and were dedicated to the memory of Jimmie and Ann's eldest son, William, who died just before his 23rd birthday in 1988, as a result of injuries sustained in a car crash. As well as being open to the public, the courts are also home to Trottiscliffe Tennis Club - a thriving club whose members come from a wide area and take part in local league competitions.

'The Wetlands', to the Trottiscliffe Society - who wanted to have a go with that. And, in turn, they helped me with a bit of hedging and things like that. It sort of became a bit of a village project which was quite fun.

The village has been very kind to me and I always want to repay that kindness. It's a very warm and friendly village where one has terrific support in times of trouble - and I have a lot to repay.

West Malling Village Hall

Linda Javens

When my Dad, Fred Gandon came home from the war, he really felt that he needed to do something. I think they lost so many years - he didn't see me until I was 3 ½, you know. He had gone away, he came back, and I think he felt he wanted to just do something... he had a lot of energy.

So, he was on the parish council and decided, "We need a village hall - this is what we need."

This, I believe, was probably the late 1950's, early 1960's. And it was decided that they would have an Oast House - they actually agreed it with the council - it was on the edge of the cricket ground. They fund raised and everything was going ahead and just a week before Dad was about to sign the lease, one of the roundels fell down.

Now, this devastated him. He just didn't know what to do about it. They couldn't rebuild it so they had to start again with fundraising for a new build. They had some wonderful carnivals which Dad instigated. And obviously a lot of other fundraising... And in about 1975 they had a brand new hall which is on the edge of the playing field - absolutely lovely! It was an achievement for all of those involved. And Dad was delighted...

Fundraising for the village hall started in 1961. The roundel of The Oast collapsed on 22 January 1971.
The hall was eventually opened on 22 March 1975 by Derek Underwood, who was a Kent and England cricketer.

DEVELOPMENTS – HOUSING AND INFRASTRUCTURE

Impact of Kings Hill, Offham
Mike Rowe

When we moved here I think jet flying had just ceased. I think there used to be 'Gloster Javelins' and they had left the airfield.

All there was when we came here was the gliding school, which was obviously very quiet... but obviously that didn't bring in much revenue, and Kent County Council - that owned the airfield - were looking for development and there was a public enquiry to consider the development of the airfield for commercial aviation, light aircraft. We fought vigorously against that because people could see that some of the flight paths might cross over the village and we fought long and hard to stop it becoming a commercial airfield.

I think the thing fell really because there wasn't a good commercial case for the aviation at the time - but we certainly objected strongly to it. As a result of that, the developers – 'Rouse(Kent)' came in and developed it into what was going to be a large commercial development with a little bit of housing - but actually what has happened is a large amount of housing and a little bit of commercial development.

The impact on Offham has been that the traffic through the village is quite intense, particularly first thing in the morning because it's a very easy shortcut for traffic coming from Sevenoaks. People who live along the village road, the Teston road, complain bitterly about the sound of the traffic from a very early hour of the morning and again in the evening - but once again there's very little we can do about it...

> The public enquiry into use of the airfield took place in the late 1980s. The Kings Hill development commenced circa 1993.

Leybourne Bypass
Kevin Wagstaff

Castle Way was getting busier and busier, and in the morning, and in the evenings, you basically couldn't cross the road. Well, actually, you could cross the road because the traffic was going so slowly that you could just walk across - because it was so busy!

There had been plans for a bypass for, oh, goodness knows how many years - but it was always one of these things where money was available from somewhere and then not - so it never sort of progressed.

Clearly, as a resident of Leybourne, making Castle Way a dual carriageway was not my favourite option and, realistically, it didn't make any sense. It would be dualling what was an old farm road.

I was on the school governers at the time and went to all the various meetings presenting on the behalf of the school, because essentially, at the intersection where the school and the church are, it would effectively be going up to each of the walls. Those who were arguing why it should be dualled were basically saying that the bypass would take away woodland and agricultural land and therefore be less harm to the environment.

We had a petition in the village that was presented... and someone from the Parish Council went to the meetings to present that.

Fortunately, from my perspective, common sense prevailed and the bypass was built.

> The Leybourne Bypass was opened in October 2006.

Leybourne Lakes Country Park
David Thornewell

The biggest thing as a Councillor I'm proud of is the establishment of Leybourne Lakes Country Park... which - although wrongly called that name - is entirely in Larkfield and Snodland.

When I was Leader of the Borough Council, an officer said to me, "You always wanted a country park - and we can deliver you a country park if you want. You'll have to agree to find some finances so that the Leybourne Lakes houses, at one end, finance the country park".

So the rest of the country park was financed by those houses without any contribution from any council tax or anything like that.

So Berkeley Homes bought the whole site of the country park, which had been the marshes, was later gravel and sand pits... and we now have the country park down there. And when I go down there and see how well used it is, I always think that's a worthwhile achievement.

Leybourne Lakes Country Park

The first sand and gravel pits in the area were dug in the late 1920s. Excavation continued through to the 1960s.

The Leybourne Lakes Country Park officially opened in 2003.

R.A.F. and West Malling
Mrs M. A. West

The R.A.F. was still at the airfield, with married quarters and as they shopped in West Malling, everyone was glad of them.

By this time, a trickle of outside people began to move in and started to object to things such as the church bells, cockerels crowing and other rustic noises. They also came knocking on doors, wanting to rid the town of the R.A.F. They received no sympathy from me.

The R.A.F. moved out in the 1960s. Before they went, they indulged in a load of low flying overhead. They dived bombed, so to speak. My mother, daughter and self did our own diving under the dining room table!

They moved, and the Americans moved in - very good for 'The Five Pointed Star'. They too moved on, and, apart from a skeleton staff of R.A.F., it was a redundant airfield.

SWAG, RAFA and West Malling Airfield,
Linda Javens

I was born during the war, so my first memory, really, of the airfield, was when I went to my senior school and many of my friends were living there because their parents were stationed there - so I was able to visit...

The next time that I was really involved with it was going to the dances as I got old enough.

In 1981, the 'We'll Meet Again' films were filmed there and round about that time they used to have very, very big air shows called 'The Warbirds' and that was fantastic - thousands used to come to that from all around. They had the 'Sally B' flying from there. We used to have a fly-pass by 'The Vulcan'. It was a wonderful day out.

My husband had been in the Air Force - not locally, but, as a family, we just loved aircraft. So then, all of a sudden, the Council decided they were going to sell the area and make a business park and that caused great upset. Now, I'm not saying everybody felt the same way, but we were upset about it.

I think a lot of local people felt that there was going to be a very large airport there if they didn't close it because the runway was magnificent.... It would take large aircraft.

But we felt that if they could have just done something alongside such an historical and lovely airport ... apparently Gibson flew from there and that was his favourite airport.

Ted Bates was a glider pilot up there and he

had instructed The Cadets, which was a lovely facility. We got chatting to him and he felt the same way as we did. So, with his instigation, we formed 'S.W.A.G.' – Save West Malling Airfield Group. We campaigned and we tried to make people aware that the impact was going to be devastating.

We used to go to meetings but the Council were always just one step ahead of us and there were people, obviously, that didn't agree with us.

We really felt that they weren't understanding what was going to happen, but unfortunately, to no avail, it was sold and the development started.

Now a strange thing sort of happened after that. We'd become very friendly with

very like-minded people and a lot of them belonged to the Royal Air Forces Association. We didn't have one locally so we all decided that we would start a new branch, called the' Aylesford and Malling Branch', for the welfare of past and present serving servicemen who need some sort of monetary help.

So something came out of a disappointment... which was good.

> **The 618 Volunteer Gliding School, West Malling**
> The Air Cadet Gliding School ran at West Malling from 1995 – 1964 and was the last RAF unit to operate from what was RAF West Malling.

> Save West Malling Airfield Group was formed to fight against the development of the site. After their campaign, some members of SWAG who had strong links and interests in the RAF formed a new branch of the Royal Air Forces Association in October 1995 - the Aylesford and Malling Branch. RAFA supports the welfare of past and present servicemen.

> The Kings Hill and West Malling airfield site, on the high plateau between Mereworth and Wateringbury in the south, and East and West Malling in the north, was largely agricultural into the early 20th century having been owned in earlier centuries by Malling Abbey and the Boscawen, Fane, Twisden and Wells families. There was a landing ground among the fields during the First World War and this became a private airfield in 1930, named Maidstone Airport in 1932. During the Second World War it became RAF West Malling, and after the war a US Naval Air Station, closing to the military in 1969. It housed Vietnamese then Ugandan Asian refugees in the 1970s, while air displays and gliding continued there in the 1970s and '80s. It was sold by Kent County Council to a United States property developer, Rouse Kent (now Liberty). Development of the site into what is now known as 'Kings Hill' started in 1989. The original plan was for a high tech business park to cover 647 acres. The development has now changed to mainly housing.

West Malling Airfield

Molly Potts

I remember when we moved here there used to be a Spitfire, not flying, but it used to be outside the gates there. That got towed up to Leuchars in Scotland I believe.

Nobody really wanted the airfield development at the time. When I moved here I remember somebody telling me it was really up to be an open prison - but that obviously didn't happen. Then the small company called Met

Air was up there. They used to do private jets for Arabs and such - and they had a concrete runway and everything put down there.

Occasionally, there'd be a boot fair up there.

Then they filmed a programme called 'We'll Meet Again', with Suzanna York up there. It was about the Yanks in Britain, a sort of love story really, supposed to be set in Norfolk but it was up at the airfield. They had the 'Sally

B', which is the B17 bomber keep taking off and coming back and the rest were a load of cardboard cut outs!

And then Gary Newman, the pop star, started an interest and every year there for ten years they had the great 'Warbirds' Air Show, where they used to come from all over the place you know - World War 2 planes, even World War 1 planes - because that's how the airfield started - as an overflow from Detling, which was the airfield.

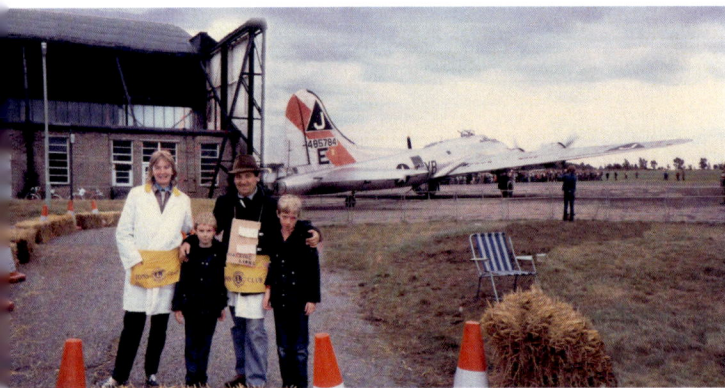

**Mike Rowe and family at
'The Great Warbirds Air Display' in 1983**

'The Great Warbirds Air Display' ran from 1982 until 1991 and was produced by seventies pop star Gary Numan.

Widening of the road in Addington

Audrey Marsh

So what you now know as the Trottiscliffe Road was much narrower.

With the coming of the sand business they had to widen it to take the lorries. There were many, many lorries then going backwards and forwards and they had to have room to pass. So that's when the road was widened and when the nasty bend in the East Street area - they had to straighten it out as much as they could. And that's why at the corner just after East Street, there is a triangle and you can see the old road quite clearly.

That is how we got our road widened - because they wanted the sand in the car industry to polish the cars. Silica sand is very, very fine you know... you could blow it away!

It was in the heyday of the Minis...

And the bridge over the stream... that went at the same time. It's rather a pity, because it was rather pretty and we used to play 'poo sticks' with the children there. You could drop the sticks in one side and run across what was quite a small road and see them come out the other side!

The sandpits between Addington and Trottiscliffe began to be exploited during the 1930's.
The ultra fine silica sand in this area is particularly valuable for foundry work, but the coarser varieties were used when the M20 motorway was being constructed during the late 1960's. They have been owned by a number of different mineral extraction companies over the decades. Some are still in operation, and others have been returned to farmland.

The little bridge mentioned in Audrey's story is called Plowenders Bridge

Javelins at Kings Hill

Dr Richard Morrice

I have strong memories of living up at Kings Hill, though I'm not sure we called it that then.

My father was a flight commander on 85 Squadron and the family story was that, on visiting with his squadron commander, prior to moving the squadron in, they reported that the runway was long enough for Javelin night fighter's to land but not for them to take off again.

Their warning was not heeded by the Air Ministry and they duly landed but then had to be dismantled and taken out rather ignominiously on St Marys (transporters). The air station then closed, or rather was passed to US use. That at least was the family story but my brother tells me that my father's log books show that he spent a year happily flying Javelins in and out of West Malling, from August 1959 to August 1960. The official story is that the aerodrome passed out of RAF use because of the increasing noise of fighter jets. Certainly, most such air stations in the south east had closed by 1970.

EARLY MEMORIES

Birling Manor
Margaret Ivell

Oh yes, I've many memories of the ruins of Birling Manor, because it was, for us children, an adventure playground. We didn't understand the dangers of playing there of course. We would go down to what we called 'the dungeons', but it was the cellars really. We'd climb the walls, and there were still certain parts that were still accessible as rooms. I remember one room like a turret which had lots of stuffed birds and the glass domes in it, and wax flowers in there. And in a garage was a car. Why it sat there all through the war, I don't know! And there was a horse drawn sledge in one of them, as well. And over the main door of the manor was a bull, which is part of the insignia of the Nevills, and the boys would prove themselves by climbing up and sitting on the back of the stone bull. Goodness knows why, but they did!

It was a great place to go and play, and there were wonderful rhododendrons and lilacs in there to see, as well. So yeah, it was a good place to be when you were small. And there was no television... only a radio. And as the farm we lived in didn't have any electricity, it was what we used to call an 'accumulator radio', and you'd have to take the battery to be recharged to a Mr Burtonshaw in Snodland.'

Birling Manor after the fire.

Birling Manor burned down in 1917.

Butcher's Lane, Mereworth
Ann Fisher

Before I moved into the village, one of my mother's sisters lived in the village, and she actually worked in the butcher's shop. And prior to me going to school, I used to go to work with her on certain days. So I have quite vivid memories of being in the butcher's shop. And just up the lane from there, there was what you'd now call an abattoir - it's where they used to actually kill the animals. And it didn't have any street lighting and it used to be quite scary, when I was at secondary school, coming up the bottom part of the lane, past what I remembered used to be the abattoir.

Deliveries, West Malling
Ron Martin

The one thing I do remember from that period is that mother had a lot of people delivering. Obviously we had milk delivered... the Co-op Bakery delivered in West Malling, and the grocer from Snodland delivered. There was the oil man from Larkfield - candles and paraffin oil - and the milk lady - she always used to call and mum always had a cup of tea for them.

Then the lady who delivered the milk - horse and cart – said, "Would I like to help at the weekends?" So I used to go and help her.

She used to have a round from the dairy, down the High Street, along the London Road, through to Offham and then all around Offham. That was lovely you know... I used to get a chance to drive the horse and cart on the way home.

And then we had Mr Clist - he had a little shop in Police Station Road, and he had a three wheeled van and he used to come round - vegetables, sweets and cigarettes! I always remember because mum used to smoke in those days, but she only had 20 cigarettes a week.

Early Memories, West Malling
Diane Hart

I was born in Norman Road in my grandmother's house - just opposite the cricket field there. So the earliest memories I've got are when my baby brother was born, when I was four. And the Badminton Hall was there, and then the council sold it, and it was a cinema, and that's where you'd take your baby to be weighed and get the orange juice and the cod liver oil and malt.

I can remember the Coronation Tea we had in there and all the flags - they went right across the road from the Badminton Hall to the houses and every child in the village (and there was a lot of children then) - we all had an afternoon tea and a Coronation mug to celebrate the Coronation.

We used to have loads of Sports Days in the cricket field. You've probably heard of Mac Macey - we named Macey's Meadow after him. He used to come down and he'd whiten all the things out and we'd have races and it was always a good fun day. And August Bank Holidays we always used to have a Flower Show, where people used to put their vegetables and flowers in the show. And there was a Baby Show as well - my youngest won the Baby Show one year.

We used to have the fair come. I remember going down the helter skelter with no mat and my dad taking me to nurse Usmer next door, and I remember lying across his lap and crying and she was getting the splinters out.

> The 'Coronation' was the celebration of the Coronation of Queen Elizabeth II in 1953.

New Housing Estate, West Malling
Diane Hart

When we moved up, this was a strawberry field and this was the first estate built after the war. Mum and Mrs Smith had the Show Houses and they were the only two houses on the estate that had tiles all over the ground floor.

But when I came here, there used to be cows and sometimes there were sheep - it's all arable now... Years ago there'd be corn, but then one year you'd have all sprouts or peas. But the cattle gradually went and the farm - Fartherwell Farm. There was a manager on the farm – Ted and I played up there with his children. I mean that was our playground really.

We'd go out all day and my mum never worried because we were all safe. She'd pack us a bag of sandwiches and a bottle of water and we'd go up the fields and we'd make camps out of the straw bales. We played out all the time - there was no playground or anything because that was all allotments down there.

I remember one day my mum had gone up the garden to get the washing in and she started shouting. There was a paling fence separating our garden from a little wood up there and we'd forgot to put the fence back and the sheep had come through into the garden. So I can remember mum shouting about that and saying we weren't to go up there anymore.

But things have just changed so much. There were children in every house. There was a hopscotch season and a skipping season and a two ball season. Mum used to say, "Don't play with the ball up against the wall, Dad's on night work", so there was weeks you had to be quiet.

Fartherwell Hall

Fartherwell Hall was a magnificent house and private estate that had been owned by the Wingfield Stratford family. Local people can remember the family used to travel around in a horse-drawn coach. When the last person died in the c. 1950s there was nobody to inherit the estate so it went up for auction and all the items of the house were sold off. The house was demolished and shortly afterwards the first phase of the Fartherwell housing estate was developed. Only the original stables now remain.

The allotments mentioned in Diane's story were developed for housing in 1974 and are now called 'Woodland Close'.

Scrumping Apples, Cows and Primary School, Larkfield

David Thornewell

I remember Church Farm belonging to the Chapman's and the cows used to go down New Hythe Lane to graze on the marshes and my mother didn't like cows - she was frightened of cows.

So if on the way to school the cows came out, we had to wait until they had gone down the road ahead and were clear before we could continue the journey to school.

When I went to the Primary School, Larkfield was very small - it was mostly agricultural land. My recollection is there were about 124 /125 pupils in the school and when I used to go home and talk to my mother about who there was at school, she would know most of those people. So you couldn't do anything wrong on the way to school because one of the parents of one of these people would tell your mother that, " Your David's been doing such and such", because everyone knew everyone else!

Where Martin Square is… that was an orchard with a public foot path running through it, and I can remember, scrumping

St. Martin's Square, Larkfield

the apples from the trees... and Mr Lane used to look after this orchard.

He couldn't run very fast, so you could beat him out the other side of the orchard before he caught you! And the foot path that led to that orchard still exists (the first part of it) next to Morrison's from the A20.

My dad used to work at the paper mills down New Hythe Lane and going to school, there were always Reeds lorries going up and down the lane with reels of paper on the lorries - and there were people walking to work and lots of people cycling to work. There were very few people having cars going to the mills. I was born in 1948, so we're talking about 1953 onwards.

Albert E Reed opened his first paper mill at Tovil in 1894 and came to New Hythe in the 1920s eventually expanding from the river right up to where the M20 now runs. Around 8,000 were employed on the site.

Shops, West Malling

Diane Hart

I remember going up to do my mum's shopping and it was the in the International Stores and in the middle it had this wooden kiosk with all glass round it and a lady sat in there and that's where you paid your bill. And in the front of the counter there was all the biscuit tins… broken biscuits. But if you had broken biscuits you could have more because they weren't so expensive.

And I remember getting the sugar and the tea in the blue paper bags. It was a thick blue paper and they used to stick the top down.

I can remember going into the butchers which was just up the road. The International Stores was where the travel agents is now. Then down Swan Street was the butcher and the manager was Mr Fagg. And my mum worked there in the war so she knew all the different cuts of meat and everything. I can remember going in there with sixpence and getting an 'H' bone to make some soup. I can remember as clear as anything…

High Street, West Malling.

We had about five butchers in West Malling at one time and they were all busy. It was a busy thriving town. And then in the '60's, at one point, we had eleven shops empty. And then the frozen food place came and then Tesco's took over. Of course, when you've got a young family and money's short - you shop for your purse - everybody went to Tesco's. They all gravitated there because they were cheaper than anywhere else and even though you could see it coming - one by one the shops closed.

The frozen food store mentioned in Diane's story was Cartier's Superfoods - a Kent based supermarket chain, active from the early to the late 1970s. Tesco acquired 17 outlets affiliated with Cartier's Superfoods.

The Fire Station, West Malling

Diane Hart

I remember the old Fire Station... And it had the siren on top - and that was the air raid siren. So when you heard that go off, you knew there was a fire somewhere.

And I can remember my dad taking me up there to watch the firemen come in and get the fire engine out.

There was a man up there and his name was Shuffle and he'd stand in the middle of the High Street. The men didn't have cars, they only had push bikes and they'd come from each road on their push bikes. And he'd stand and they'd get off, leave the bike running on its own. He'd grab the bike and put it up against the wall... And that's how all the men got there.

West Malling Fire Station circa 1898

West Malling Fire Station was established in 1898 and continued to function until the early 1970s, when local fire services were transferred to Larkfield and the site of the Fire Station and the George Inn were cleared to build the Cartier's frozen food store (later Tesco).

EDUCATION

Bricks, Offham Primary School

Christina Rogerson

When we had our extension, parents, children and staff were asked if they would like to buy a brick in memory of the extension. And I have my own brick that's set into the path and so do a lot of the former pupils who were attending the school at the time. It's just along the corridor from the library... There's a little pathway and it's edged with these bricks in commemoration of the extension. And, of course, they will be there forever... well hopefully forever, but for the foreseeable future anyway!

Children hiding under their desks, 70th Anniversary Celebrations at Ryarsh School.

In around 2003, ninety four 'named' bricks were laid within the grounds of Offham School.

History Repeats Itself at Ryarsh School

Louise Parfitt

The school was built and opened in 1941 when the village schools became too small for the amount of children that they were then taking in - there were a lot of evacuees moving down from London.

To celebrate the Diamond Jubilee, the 60th year, we had a war time theme to our summer fete and tried to dress accordingly... We had lots of land girls, army officers and lots of events - the children did displays in the arena which reflected war time fun and games.

We've just recently celebrated our 70th anniversary, and we decided to go back to 1941 and the war years, and every day throughout the whole week was dedicated to a year of the war - World War II. It was all very much done without the children knowing what was going to be happening. The school just sent letters home describing what the children needed to wear when they turned up on Monday morning and that they would be wearing that throughout the week. Over the weekend staff emptied all of the classrooms of all of the electrical equipment,

Louise Parfitt, 70th Anniversary Celebrations at Ryarsh School.

computers and white boards. We taped up all the windows and reverted everything back as much as we could to the 40s and particularly 1941/42, to when the school was first opened. All the staff dressed up accordingly and we went back to ringing the bell as opposed to blowing a whistle at the end of break and lunchtime, and we've actually kept that tradition now.

We had a really fun time. The children learned so much. We tried to follow each stage as the war was progressing, in a sensitive assembly in the mornings, which all of the children could relate to and understand. And we finished off the week with a street party. Unfortunately it rained and we had to have it in the hall but it was all banners and cakes and all the children brought in plates of sandwiches and jelly and lemonade and we had a really good time.

Throughout the week there was always something different going on. The children made gas masks and we actually blew the

siren. We still have an air raid shelter at Ryarsh School and we cleaned that out and made it out to look like a shelter and the children, when they heard the siren, depending on whose turn it was, would rush to the air raid shelter and we'd shut them in there. But it wasn't done in a way to frighten them and they really enjoyed it. Either that or they had to get under their tables and we've got pictures in school of them all hiding under the tables with their paper gas masks on.

One of the highlights of the week was a visit by 'The Home Front Bus'- an old double-decker bus which has been converted into a fantastic mobile learning centre about life during WWII.

So many of the children said that the memories of that week will stick with them and made comments like, "We really, really enjoyed that - it was really good fun!"

> Ryarsh Primary School, Birling Road, Ryarsh opened in 1941. The first pupils came from Ryarsh National School which was situated on Old School Lane and had been built in 1869. Pupils also came from the village school in Birling when it closed and from Addington School when it closed c. 1943. The original school on Old School Lane has now been converted into two cottages.

Mereworth School in the 1960s.

Marion Regan

It was a very good school. We had a lot of school children from the AMQ (Airmens' Married Quarters) and OMQ (Officers' Married Quarters) up at the airfield. In the early years there were many American children there, because the Americans were stationed there. Later they were just RAF, and a lot of the children had fathers who were serving in Aden. So we always did a very good trade in foreign coins, because they always had lots of foreign ones. So it was a big school, because there were quite a lot of children from the West Malling Airfield.

And there were some very memorable teachers in my time at Mereworth Primary. There was Miss Curd, who taught there for

many, many years and has only recently died in her 90's. And she lived just opposite the 'Duke Without a Head' at Pizien Well. She was a very good, influential teacher. And the Headmaster in my time there was Mr Cook, who used to hang a white board outside his office if we were allowed to go in the field, which was the most exciting thing we were allowed to do... if the white board was up, we could go in the field!

Boys and girls were segregated and after the age of seven, we played in different playgrounds. I think that changed in the latter years I was there. Yes... a very happy school!

Mereworth School, 1931

> 'The Duke Without a Head' public house on the Tonbridge Road, Wateringbury, was demolished some years ago and the site is now occupied by houses.

> When the RAF left the airfield, the AMQ, situated on the west side of the A228, became a council estate. The OMQ, to the east, was developed and sold off and is now known as 'Kate Reed Wood'.

School - Ryarsh and West Malling
Margaret Gadd

First of all I went to private school on the London Road - Miss Bance - she was great fun. She was very elderly and she'd been the Headmistress at Ryarsh School, and she ran a private school for a bit until she retired. And then I went to Ryarsh Primary - the headmistress, Miss Andrews - she was very good. And she would take us out when we got a certain age and she walked us a stretch of the Pilgrims Way and told us all about what went on - Beckett and the rest of it, and the 'Canterbury Tales'. She read us this sort of dispersed version of the 'Canterbury Tales' and took us down to Canterbury so that we could see the end result and then encouraged us to write our own version - which I always think was very forward thinking - because you don't always get all these sorts of things in schools now.

She made it her business to know what was going on locally. And anything that went on - we were always included in, which I always think was quite good.

> Miss Bance ran a small private school in her home on London Road for about ten years after retiring from Ryarsh School.
> The Pilgrims Way was the name later given to a prehistoric trackway running from Winchester in Hampshire to Folkestone in Kent. From medieval times it was used by pilgrims visiting the shrine of Saint Thomas Becket in Canterbury Cathedral. Locally, the Pilgrims Way can still be walked along the North Downs above Trottiscliffe, Ryarsh and Birling.
> The famous 'Canterbury Tales', written by Geoffrey Chaucer in the late 14th century, is presented as part of a story-telling contest between a group of pilgrims as they travelled from Southwark to Canterbury, the prize being a free meal at the Tabard Inn, Southwark on their return.

School, East Malling
Leslie Fox

At school we had four classrooms - two of them were in the main hall. There was a Major Acton as the Master. Mrs Rullerford was one teacher, a Mrs Wright - she was the second. There was a man teacher but he was a bit unpleasant, he used to throw chalks at all the boys when they were talking. And there was a Miss Wigan... lots of Wigans in East Malling then! They owned Blacklands, Clare House up the top of Clare Lane. I think they've built a school or houses all behind there now...

There was a young school teacher who used to give the girls a little caning now and again if they didn't behave - she'd got her cane behind the cupboard!

There was long forms and long desks, so once you got in the desk, you were all trapped behind the other pupils!

> Clare House is a Grade I Listed Palladian Mansion built circa 1797 and designed by and for the paper maker John Larkin. It was later the seat of the Wigans family.

Teacher Training, East Malling
Douglas Rabjohn

At the end of the war there was a great shortage of male teachers and there was also a shortage of qualified teachers of all sorts - because many men teachers, those who weren't called up for the army, had gone on way beyond retirement age.

Obviously, when the war ended, they wanted to get out of teaching and enjoy what was left of their lives.

There was a scheme called 'The Emergency Teacher Training Scheme'. I applied to that and was successful. I went down to the teacher training college at Eastbourne and did the 13 months course and passed it alright and became a qualified teacher - but with an extended period of probation. We had to teach for two years, were frequently examined and had to attend night school. I did my probation at the school here in East Malling and I didn't leave East Malling - I just continued on here for the rest of my working life until I retired in 1983.

This is a class photo from Mr Rabjohn's class at theChapel St school in summer 1959. The class spanned twoschool years, taught together.

Mr Rabjohn's class of 1959, Chapel Street School, East Malling

Manningham House, Infants School, East Malling, 1965

East Malling School was founded c. 1846. It was first sited at what is now Manningham House in Chapel Street and moved to Mill Street in 1959. Mr Rabjohn's class was one of the first to move to the new school. Mr Rabjohn became Deputy Head teacher of the school.

Trottiscliffe School

Ann Kemp

The school during our time here has had its ups and downs. The numbers of children have fluctuated enormously and we had the very traumatic experience of our school being up for closure.

The village got together, and we launched the most tremendous campaign and saved our school, and we are delighted that it remained open and the numbers are now on the up - and we have a new, wonderful Head Teacher and the school is thriving.

It's always been a focal point of the village... for a lot of the community activities... The village fête and the fireworks and a lot of the social life of the village in the past were centred on the school.

We had a terrific fundraising event to raise money, to add a classroom, when that was needed. And we had a television programme come down and they had a big sort of jumble sale that they held in the village hall, and it was all televised.... which raised a lot of money for the school and was organised by the Parents Association.

Trottiscliffe has had its own school since the 19th century. The present buildings were erected during the 1960's on a site very close to the original structure, which is now a private home. The number of children on the roll has fluctuated over the years, and during the 1980's dropped, for a year or so, down to the mid forties. Although it had risen well above this by the turn of the 21st century, it was threatened with closure during 2006, as part of a rationalisation of small rural schools. As Ann says, Trottiscliffe School now has the facilities to take it forward robustly.

West Malling Primary School and The Abbey, West Malling

Sister Mary Mark

Sometime in the late 1960's somebody who used to live in the Gatehouse was coming back from the station when she saw some little boys fiddling with the wall. It turned out that the two or three little boys were setting off squibs* in the boundary wall in an effort to dislodge some of the stones. Alison said, "You know, we don't do that sort of thing", and shooed them off.

Mother Abbess wrote to the Headmaster of our local school appealing to him to remedy this if he could. Mr McIntosh… who was a dear replied that he felt sure it couldn't possibly have been any of his boys, but just in case it was, he would like to bring a group of children to sing Christmas carols to us in reparation and to meet some of the nuns.

This became an annual event for many years, but more recently the children have come in the summer, generally with a project in hand.

*A squib is a miniature explosive device that resembles a tiny stick of dynamite in appearance though it has considerably less explosive power. Colloquially used for a small firework it is also called a "banger".

West Malling Church of England Primary School in Norman Road was opened in 1954, replacing a boys' school on the High Street and a school for girls and infants in Churchfields (the latter continued as an infants' school until 1975).

West Malling Schools

Ron Martin

I actually had a term at Leybourne School and then, because of the travelling down there, mother moved us to West Malling into the little primary school by the church. I always remember our third of a pint of milk in the mornings… And when you first went there as a junior you had a rest in the afternoon on a little camp bed!

Then at the age of seven you went to the boys' school – the boys did - and that was eye opener actually, because at that time the boys were there still to the age of 14. There was no secondary education when I first went there. And some of the games that were played - Oh my God they were rough and ready! British Bulldog - that was a bit rough! And then there were the horseback fights with the bigger boys having the little boys on their backs and wrestling to the ground, all in a playground which was really hard!

Our teacher is still alive - Miss Wakefield. She was a marvel, she was – I think she awakened a lot of things in us, those that were receptive anyway.

West Malling Boys School, circa 1919.

Actually I did a little talk for the primary school children last year. It was about 70 years since I started at the primary school and I actually told them what we did, you know. And two of my memories of the shops on the way to school…

When we used to go to the primary school at

the top, we'd come home and occasionally we'd get an ice-cream in the dairy - where the Abbotsley Veterinary Surgery is now. You'd go in and there was a flagstone floor and it was cool and you used to have the little circular ice-creams in their carton surround.

And when we were at the boys' school, and people laugh about this... Frosty mornings, if we had any money, which wasn't very often, we used to go to Briggs Bakery, where the bakery restaurant is and buy a bread roll straight out of the oven. We'd eat the inside and put the outsides over our ears to warm them up!

Working at Offham Primary School

Christina Rogerson

I first came to Offham Primary School in December 1988. ...The then Headteacher was away, he was teaching in Oregon in the United States, and we had an American teacher - Susan Larfield who came to the school in his place.

When I started, Sue Robertson was the acting Head and she certainly made me feel at home. She showed me around and said, "Would I like the job?" and I said, "Yes please, I would!", and I've been here ever since... which is quite a long time.

During that time, I've become even more attached to the school...

I think that Offham School has changed... of course it has. When I first joined the school there were only 58 children on roll. Now we usually have up to 210 children and obviously

we've had to expand...

We've had a couple of extensions during the time I've been here...

In 1996 we had the new hall, then in 2003, we had an extension to the school and we had the official opening of that extension in 2004 to which local residents, governors and certain dignitaries were invited - like The Right Honourable Sir John Stanley - he attended... it was quite a busy affair.

And they could see how the school was many years ago and what had happened to it, and the reasons why it needed to expand - obviously because there were more children needing more places at school.

What hasn't changed is the atmosphere... you know, the ethos of the school.... I think from being a very small school with 58 on roll, to having 210 children on roll... that's always remained the same... and I really do feel it's a wonderful place...

Offham School was built in 1875 and opened on 3 April 1876. The Head teacher's house was built at the same time. A Miss Rosanna Philpott was the first Head teacher and she worked at the school until December 1876.
The original school, known as Offham Board School, had one room and had 68 children on roll. Children attended until they were old enough to leave school and were charged for attending school until education was made free in 1892.

Offham School

HISTORICAL BUILDINGS AND SITES OF INTEREST

Addington Stones

Joan Bygrave

I came to live in the village in 1966 and took on the land that has two Neolithic tombs on it. I must admit I knew very little about early prehistory at that time, but I had to learn very quickly as I discovered that people really wanted to come and see these places.

So, for all this time I've been welcoming people to come and have a look at the tombs and explain to them the significance of them. A lot people come and I get to learn about interesting things!

All sorts of people including Jools Holland come - you wouldn't expect a top musician to be interested in Neolithic tombs, but he's not the only person - there have been people in the academic world…

So I never really know who's going to turn up on the doorstep. Sometimes there are rather odd people like ley liners, Baha'i chanters and earth energy people.

I am willing to welcome anybody as long as they don't do anything to damage the tombs. Ultimately, I am responsible to English Heritage for their wellbeing. There is a field warden who has to be given access whenever he or she arrives, and if they find anything untoward about the place, or how I am keeping it, then I am the one who could go to prison or have a £2,000 fine. So I do restrict the access by asking to know where people come from and keeping a visitors' book. Of course, when you see 'Mickey Mouse' entered in it you know you are being conned!

But equally I have some control over what happens. There have been times in the past when I didn't have a gate and gave unlimited access - when I'd go out to the field where the main tomb stands and find people having a picnic at 9 o'clock at night in the better weather. That's disconcerting when people haven't asked for access and you don't know who they are or what they are going to do - so it beholds me to be a bit wary about it.

Equally, it's been a wonderful way of meeting people - particularly now I am getting older and don't necessarily go out to meet them. So - an interesting life!

There are two tombs and they appear to be orientated to the Mid-Summer Solstice and the Mid-Winter Solstice. So they may be two of the first that went up in the valley and there

The Chestnuts Neolithic Tomb, Addington taken in 2003.

Addington's two chamber tombs, the Chestnuts and Addington Long barrow, are amongst the earliest in the country. They are believed to have been constructed around 3,700 B.C., by early Neolithic farmers, on a site previously used by Mesolithic hunter gatherers. It is accepted that there was very little time between the two groups of settlers, so perhaps there was conflict, but maybe integration?

"Ley lines" are supposed alignments between places or landscape features. These invisible lines are believed to have been used by early man to link burial chambers and other monuments to each other or to important features in the landscape. The term was coined in 1921 by amateur archaeologist, Alfred Watkins, who put forward a thesis that they were used as a means of safely crossing a landscape. His theory is still not universally accepted. However, holding a dowsing rod amongst the Addington megaliths, even by someone who has never held one before, can be quite interesting!

"Earth energies" is another term for what a dowsing rod is seeking, including water.

has recently been a five year project to look at the prehistoric landscape in the Medway valley. And certainly they have increased significance now, because they do appear to be the ones which were perhaps important to these early settlers, because they were linked to an agricultural cycle and warned how the seasons were going to change. These people were settling in an area and using their environment instead of being hunter gathers, moving through the landscape - they were getting more community minded. There was probably conflict because originally, hunter gathers could go where they liked and now people were saying, "This bits mine! Keep off!" So, there was probably a lot of conflict... We know very little really.

The Historical Buildings of Kings Hill

David Murray

I used to know a chap called Squadron Leader Dennis Jackson who was part of the Malling Airfield Group – he was trying to get a memorial put up... which through their efforts did happen - and it's straight outside of the Community Centre. In fact, that site is exactly on the site of the old Station Headquarters and the Community Centre is actually on the site of the old Guard Room.

I can remember that the road that goes down is in exactly the same place. The building on the left which I think is Genzyme now was the Sergeants' Mess... I think they've obviously converted the inside. The buildings on the right in Churchill Square were the airmen's accommodation... which is now being used for small businesses... but the actual infrastructure, if you walked into it... you could visualize what it'd be like in the forties, when it was an active airfield.

So a lot of the infrastructure is still here as far as the buildings are concerned, but it's been developed into something more 20th century... so it's brilliant the way that it's been done. There was talk of the big hangars being converted or used for sports facilities, but... they went... and all the concrete's been pulled up from the runways... but it still exists in as much as it's probably under all the houses as hardcore 'cause it was all dug up and crushed down. So West Malling Airfield still exists, in part or in pieces shall we say!

But I really do support the concern from West Malling over the facilities that were from the war. A lot of them obviously are still here although if you didn't know the history you wouldn't necessarily notice unless it was pointed out. But you can see from the layout and you can still see some of the markings on the Tonbridge and Malling building... ...you can see some of the camouflage and I believe it did get hit with a bomb and if you look at a certain place, you can see part of the roof, where it had been replaced. So, if you really look... there is some of the history still here.

There is still a tower, in Tower View, which was used as an observation tower during the war, with a gun emplacement adjacent to it. The buildings are partially hidden in the trees to the right of Tower View as you enter the development, near the obelisk.

Recently, the central area was redeveloped to show off the newly refurbished Control Tower which is to become a Heritage Centre, coffee shop and small business premises; using two 'pods' built - one on either side of the existing control tower.

The Memorial outside the Kings Hill Community Centre

In 2013, there was a fly past of a Spitfire to mark the 70th Anniversary of the Dam Busters Raid; the connection being that Wing Commander Guy Gibson VC DSO DFC, had been stationed at Kings Hill during the war and had commented on liking RAF West Malling. Wing Commander Guy Gibson became a household name after a raid on the German dams and is remembered at Kings Hill by a road named after him and these words on a brass plate by the entrance to the Tonbridge and Malling Council offices, previously the Officers Mess:
"Of all the airfields in Great Britain here, many say including myself, we have the most pleasant."

The Twitch Inn, West Malling

Molly Potts

Planning permission had been put in to make it houses at the back and apartments in the actual mansion. The Twitch Inn was a stumbling point as far as planning permission was concerned. It had been offered to RAFA, if they would like it - because of the RAF connection.

The Twitch Inn had been used as an officers' mess during World War 2 and the ceiling was covered in graffiti of their signatures. Also, on one of the walls, David Langton - who actually was a squadron leader but he'd been a cartoonist with the Daily Herald – he'd put cartoons of a bomb ditching procedure and several drawings of mermaids and glamour girls and things on the walls.

Anyway, after we'd had the meeting, I heard myself say, "Why don't we have it?"

Bernard (Tyson) looked at bit cross eyed and said, "What us?"

I said, "Well, we've always wanted a heritage centre or a centre that was ours".

So, the first meetings were held in my house with the property developers - they were a company called Raven Group. They then sold it on to Beechcroft.

Of course, once they got planning permission - things really moved then.

Negotiations for planning permission at Douces Manor took place in March 2004. The Twitch Inn, Malling Heritage Centre, opened in November 2010 and is managed by volunteers from the Malling Society.

The Malling Society was founded in 1965 with the main aims of stimulating public interest in the good appearance and community of West Malling, preserving local buildings and places of historic interest, and protecting the surrounding countryside. The Society also provides a programme of speakers and visits to places of interest, and holds regular exhibitions at their Heritage Centre in St. Leonard's Street and at the Clout Institute.

Malling Heritage Centre Plaque.

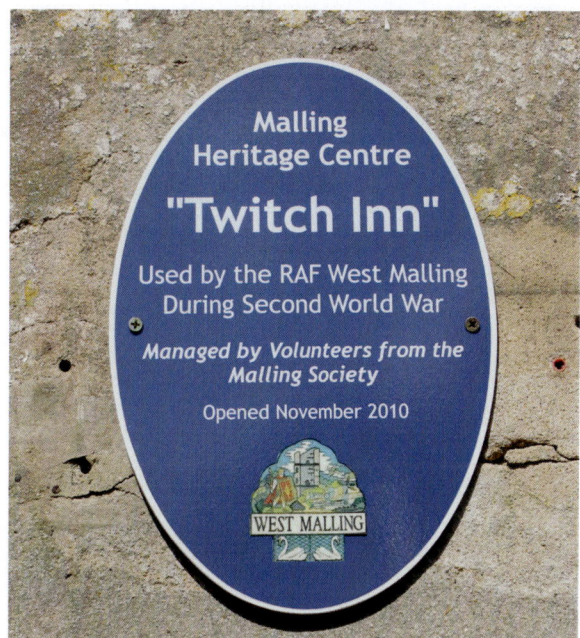

Vigo Bridge saved by the Trottiscliffe Society

Mike Towler

The bridge project landed on my plate … but it needed a lot of work done and a lot of work implies a lot of money, which we hadn't got … so we uhm'd and ah'd about it until eventually I was contacted by a member, who said, "How is the bridge project going? … because I'm prepared to sponsor it."

I said, "Well yes, that's all very well, but you know, it's going to cost a lot of money. We're going to need, at the very minimum, £3,000 pounds just to do anything with it." … and she came up with an offer of more than three times that, and indeed, she put that money into the society … and we could then go ahead…

The main work required was to replace the revetments. Thus, I designed brick structures with concrete foundations. Two factors made everything even more durable than designed. My specification was for red bricks to match the facade of the bridge. But the contractor was prepared to reduce his price if we would accept blue engineering bricks (a more expensive, much tougher, product) because he had a surplus stock that he would like to use up. Then, when they started the job they forgot to tell the excavating sub-contractor that the foundation trenches were narrow and he arrived with a wide bucket on his machine. So, excessively wide trenches were dug and duly filled with vast quantities of concrete. Those revetments are so substantial that you'd need a large bomb to demolish them.

Trosley Towers Bridge in April 2009

Mike Towler recalls that the initial success and popularity of The Trottiscliffe Society was largely due to two people: Dennis Matthews, Chairman; and Ron Saunders, Secretary. The Society was founded as an amenity society for the village, but it is now in semi-abeyance. However, at time of writing it still owns Trosley Towers Bridge. The bridge was built for Sir Sydney Waterlow, M.P., 1st Bart (1822-1906), the printer and philanthropist. In 1870 he bought large tracts of land in Fairseat, Stansted and Trottiscliffe and lived in Fairseat. He constructed carriage drives to link his land, and Vigo Bridge was built as part of this network. In the early 1880's he built Trosley Towers, renting Addington Place whilst construction took place. Sir Sydney's son inherited the estate and it was sold after Sir Philip's death in 1931. Trosley Towers was then demolished, leaving just the bridge. The bridge appeared to have descended into a very fragile state when the Trottiscliffe Society acquired it. People did worry that it might fall down!

The Wetlands, Trottiscliffe

Mike Towler

The land surrounding the village on three sides was part of the Nevill estate from Ryarsh. One of the partners was going to retire and he wanted his money out of the thing. A lot of the estate was sold, including the land on the three sides of this village, and it was all purchased by villagers in various-sized plots, some quite small. Bigger areas were purchased by other individuals, who still own them - one of whom is Ann Kemp, Borough Councillor, who promptly offered the Trottiscliffe Society the opportunity to restore, as a wildlife sanctuary, an area of wetland, which is down near the church.

In front of the church was a chain of three ponds for the Bishop's enjoyment. There was a pond for fresh water, a pond for fish, and a pond for sewage and anything else you want to get rid of. The first two ponds were filled in during the 1950s. ... And the third pond had just been used as a rubbish tip - and it was all overgrown ... a jungle ... The Trottiscliffe Society was given permission to restore that as a wildlife habitat.

In six months, nature had taken over. We'd got mallards nesting, we'd got the greatest concentration of damselflies and dragonflies that I've seen anywhere ... and butterflies - you could literally measure them by the cubic metre ... I've never seen so many.

It was wonderful, absolutely wonderful.

Tunnel at Malling Abbey

Tunnels, West Malling

Tim Baldock

There are tunnels all under West Malling High Street. Nobody's quite sure what they were used for and having a few shops in the High Street, I could go into one of them, down the cellar, into the tunnels, go under the road and come up in another shop. So, if anybody was chasing me I could disappear quite easily!

And also my father showed me the tunnel that is down at West Malling Abbey which leads out towards Leybourne Castle and its reputed there is another tunnel that leads up to St. Leonard's Keep - but nobody seems quite sure where that is.

St. Leonard's Keep and West Malling Lake were great places to grow up in. There was a spring shed with a waterwheel in and it was unmanned in those days. And as a child, a lot of us used to make camps down by the lake and the water was great fun to play around in.

Baldocks, West Malling

The Abbey tunnel has been interpreted by archaeologists as part of a medieval drain, originally carrying waste in an open sewer from the Abbey kitchens and toilet block under Swan Street to fertilise fields to the north. The tunnel collapsed within a few feet of the entrance at an unknown date; the open sewer was then filled and steps added to create a garden 'folly', probably in the 18th century.

HISTORY DISCOVERED

Ghosts, West Malling

Margaret Gadd

First of all we lived in West Malling, in Park Cottages, in St. Leonard's Street. My neighbour, who lived at number three, used to play chess at lunchtime with a friend of hers when she came home from work. This particular day she set up the chessboard before she went to work... forgot to get something out, came back in the house, went upstairs to get it, came back through the sitting room and thought, "Somebody's moved a chess piece!" She moved it, turned around to walk to the door, turned back, and another piece had been moved.

Now, this went on every time she went out the room for some weeks. And it turned out that somebody was actually playing a game of chess with her... and it wasn't her cat!... and the person won the game several times!

She wouldn't have told me this if I hadn't of had an experience myself next door...

I came back one day quite quickly, having gone out, forgot something and came back for it. I opened my front door to see somebody sitting in my armchair - I could actually see quite clearly. They were middle-aged and dressed in sort of early Victorian clothes. I remember thinking to myself as I rushed past and grabbed what I wanted, "I hope to God he's still not there when my husband gets in because he doesn't like that kind of thing!"

And we had one or two other experiences like this which went on...

Also, I was in Offham Road driving the car home one evening from my mother's when I came up to the Teston Road junction. It had been extremely warm weather and I thought at the time, "Gosh if it gets any hotter, goodness knows what we're going to do!"

As I drew up at the junction to stop and let a car to go past, I felt the air go cooler. I thought, "Oh thank goodness for that, the temperature's gone down". And then I suddenly realised I was sneezing because there was a tail of a horse that was tickling my nose and I thought, "I'm going mad here." Then I thought, "No I'm not. Good gracious me!" and I could see the shape of a knight who had ridden right through me and the car - and he went up the road in front of me, across the road, and up the ride on the other side. This was the July of 1995...

I had been talking about this earlier to some other people and also a gentleman by the name of Harold Woolston, who was the local tailor. He admits that he'd had a similar experience when he had been walking along the road in the early thirties. We also found another person whose brother had had this experience during the war. When Harold had mentioned it to people in the early thirties, he found that his grandparents and great grandparents also knew people that had these experiences. So, as it went over a hundred years, it obviously was something that had been seen on a regular basis over the time.

> Legend has it that when the four knights who murdered Thomas Becket parted, one of the knights came through West Malling, banged on the Abbey door but got no response so he rode off down West Street, turned left and went on through the woods (where there was a ride until about 20 years ago). Thomas Becket was the Archbishop of Canterbury from 1162 until his murder at Canterbury Cathedral in 1170.

Missing Portrait, Douces Manor, West Malling

Molly Potts

I did manage to find a portrait that had gone missing...

This portrait had hung on the wall in the lounge in Douces Manor and was quite expensive, done by a local artist called John Downman, who had painted Nelson after the Battle of the Nile and Georgiana, Duchess of Devonshire.

He did several local people but he also had a studio in what was known as Leicester's Fields in London - now Leicester Square. He moved on after a while, but he lived in Went House in West Malling.

I was quite concerned about this portrait and one day Mike (North) came in with a photograph on his mobile phone and said,

Thomas Augustus Douce Esq. Painted by John Downman

The missing portrait was that of Thomas Augustus Douce who was born in 1744. It was painted by John Downman in 1791.

"Is this the portrait?" and I said "Yes!"

It hadn't been documented in the book of John Downman. It had been actually recorded as 'Old Man Douce' when he was only 44, in his sixth series of collections of paintings.

After Mike gave me this information, I phoned the archivist in Norwich and I said "I think I've found the portrait" and she said, "Is it the one you've been on about for five years?" and I said "Yes!"

So I sent her an image on the computer and I said, "Also we're looking for the wooden box that the family silver used to be kept in."

She got on to the auctioneers in Cambridge – 'Chaffins', and a crime number was issued.

I'd already phoned them and said, "I think the portrait has been stolen", but of course I had no real authority.

She said that she was sending the silver chest down to Norwich, with some other stuff from the archives in London and when the van arrived with the silver chest, the portrait was on it too. So it had been given back from the auction house.

Pubs, West Malling and surrounding area

Ron Martin

My father had always said that he went on a pub crawl around West Malling and had a pint in each one. And I said, "Well that's only about twelve Dad!" He said, "No it wasn't - there were a few more about in those days!"

I then started doing research into that... how many existed in the 19th century and then disappeared at the beginning of the 20th Others were built...

So I said "I'll produce a booklet". So I did the booklet, 'West Malling Pubs'.

I got hooked on doing the history of pubs and did three more - one of East Malling, Larkfield and New Hythe; one of Addington, Trottiscliffe, Birling, Ryarsh, Leybourne and Snodland; and then just recently, one of Mereworth, Offham and West Peckham.

Family Research – Shooting in Offham

Sydney Gilliard and Josephine Crittall

Jo   I'd started my family research some years ago and there was a story that had come down through the years about a shooting in the family... and we wanted to put the story straight because nobody seemed to know exactly what happened.

Syd   We were interested to see how distorted the family story had got, because we thought we were told that it was one twin, shooting their twin sister. Jo discovered, through her research, that wasn't the case at all. There were two sets of twins in this family, but one lot were born before the incident, and the other lot were born afterwards. They were quite a large family of about thirteen children, not many of which

HISTORY DISCOVERED

survived.

It was the little girl's older brother, Frank, that had shot her - with a gun that had been left carelessly laying up against, what they called a 'hop nidget'.

Jo He was eleven years old when his sister was shot, at the age of eight, and the inquest was actually at 'The Red Lion' in Offham. I understand that the mum had gone out and the children had gone off to play, and the next thing she heard was a bang. It must have been quite high profile, I would imagine, at the time, and how dreadful for the mum…

Syd …And the brother of course.

Jo At eleven years old, you'd be old enough to remember that. It says in the article that he came running out, "Mummy I've hurt Winnie and I didn't mean to." And a policeman was walking by, and he went in and found her, dead on the floor.

The Red Lion, Offham

SHOOTING A SISTER.

SAD FATALITY AT OFFHAM.

A GUN ACCIDENTALLY DISCHARGED.

Amid all the rejoicings through Kent one pretty little village, that of Offham, near Malling, has been saddened by a terrible tragedy, by which Winifred Emily Gilliard, seven years of age, the daughter of the police constable stationed at Offham, lost her life. Mr. Buss, one of the Kent coroners, held an inquest on the body at the Red Lion on Wednesday evening, when Mr. D. C. Woodroffe was chosen foreman of the jury.—Agnes Gilliard, mother of the deceased, identified the body, and said that on Monday morning she saw the deceased and her brother Frank, aged 11, leave the house together. She had occasion to go out herself shortly afterwards, and fancied she heard a noise like a fall in the barn near by. Just then Frank ran up to her and said

"I'VE HURT WINNIE,

but I didn't mean to do it." Witness ran to the barn, and saw her little daughter lying on the floor in the centre of it. She called Mr. Morphew, a neighbour, who rendered her assistance.—Frank Gilliard said he and his sister went into the building together, and the latter directed his attention to a gun which was standing in a corner against a hop nidget. He was in the act of taking it up by the barrel, when it exploded, and his sister fell. He endeavoured to lift her up, not thinking that she was seriously injured, and then called his mother.—William Morphew, a blacksmith, also living at Offham Green, said when he arrived he could see the girl had been shot, and there was no doubt she was quite dead.—John Wagborn, of Comp, Leybourne, bailiff for Mr. Goodwin, stated that he had been scaring birds on Monday morning with the gun mentioned, and placed it temporarily, as described by other witnesses, whilst he helped to unload some hop-washing machines. The fact that he had left the gun in the barn

SLIPPED HIS MEMORY,

and it was quite half-an-hour afterwards when he went to fetch it. The accident had meanwhile happened. The trigger was very stiff to pull, and he should imagine it caught in the handle of the hop nidget.—P.C. Kitney, who was passing at the time, said there was a small wound in the child's left breast where the shot had entered, and the wound was bleeding. There was also a pool of blood where the child had laid.—The jury, after the Coroner had pointed out that the boy's story was in all probability the true version of the affair, brought in a verdict of "Accidental death," the foreman adding that they thought it was a pure accident and no blame attached to anyone.

Newspaper article, Offham Shooting.

This tragic incident took place on 21 June 1897 and involved Syd and Jo's great aunt, Winifred. Winifred's father was the local police constable in Offham at the time, which Jo thought must have raised some media interest. After more research Jo found a newspaper item in the local archives about the whole incident. Syd and Jo's great Grandfather, Gilliard, (the policeman in Offham) was posted in many villages around Kent during his police career, including Mereworth and Snodland, the latter being where he retired.

A 'hop nidget' is a triangular tool drawn behind a horse to scarify and weed the earth between the alleys of hop poles; the tool is guided from behind by a boy holding a pair of handles.

LOCAL BUSINESSES AND EMPLOYMENT

'A Briggs' Bakery, West Malling

Tony Briggs

Father died on the 13th of April, 1963, and I took over the shop then and I stayed there until 1988, when I sold it after 25 years. I had the shop as a general store but I worked in the bake house, within the bakery, as a child right up to the age of about 18 or 19 - so I had quite a lot of experience actually in the bakery. It was pretty tough going - it really was.

I enjoyed some of the work in the bake house. But some of it... the night work... doing 12-14 hours shifts as a 16, 17-year-old lad... it was pretty tough. I remember one night walking down the bake house and falling asleep and collapsing amongst all the tins and my father said, "Right. Out you go! Go walk around the town and wake yourself up!" That was when the business was coming to an end and we were working longer and longer hours. My father was having to stand men off because he couldn't afford to pay them and in the end, he declared himself bankrupt because he just couldn't carry it on.

The big boys such as 'Tiptop' and 'Wonderloaf' were coming on the scene and they slowly sold us out of business. They were flooding all our customers with sliced bread. Some were giving it away and we lost customer after customer because of this. That was the end of the baking days. They closed down quite a few shops in the area.

Arthur Briggs's Bread Cart, 1915.

Hovis introduced the wrapped sliced loaf in 1954, followed by many other 'factory' bakeries that were set up in the early 1950s, mainly by large companies already involved in flour milling. Before the advent of supermarkets they made regular deliveries direct to customers' homes, each company covering a wide area with its own fleet of delivery vans.
Following the end of wartime rationing in 1955, many small shopkeepers enjoyed a brief period of prosperity before suffering competition from companies such as Marks & Spencer, Woolworths, and self-service grocery stores – the first of the supermarkets. Bankruptcy became more common for small shopkeepers in the early 1960s.

East Malling Research Station - Climate

Malcolm Wickenden

I worked at the research station from 1960 and, in those days, there were quite a lot of people there - about 300 plus. It was a major employer in the area. And I went there at the bottom of the ladder, as a scientific assistant.

In the early days there, I worked for a Polish scientist and I was involved in work on experiments to establish the best means of protecting against spring frosts. But then suddenly the climate appeared to change and we didn't get spring frosts that caused damage for quite a number of years - so the work really came to an end.

But it was during that time that I was given

the opportunity to become the Station Met Observer. I'd been the deputy for a number of years... I've always had an interest in weather so I actually jumped at the offer and so I was there for thirty plus years as the main Met Observer.

And I expanded the station as much as I could because very little about the weather was known by anybody else there. I had free range really and I was able to do pretty much as I liked. We worked in conjunction with the 'Met Office' so the information that was collected each month went onto a form and was sent out to the Met Office, and they vetted all the data - and anything that looked untoward, you might get a questionnaire about. But we didn't tend to get many questionnaires - we made a pretty good job of things.

Planting Rootstocks at East Malling Research Station

East Malling Research Station was formed in 1913. The Met Station was set up shortly afterwards in 1914. The Research Station is currently celebrating its Centenary Year.

East Malling Research Station - Purpose, Characters and Community
John Easton

The situation when I went to the research station was that it was very much engaged in providing fruit and fruit information to growers. Because of the need to produce vast quantities of fruit after the war... there had been a lot of pressure on during the war to provide food, and that still continued. So, I was privileged to be there at a time when the research station was still expanding... and it had this reputation, quite rightly, for producing large numbers of rootstocks, which were then being sent out worldwide. It still has that reputation throughout the world even now, for the range of rootstocks... And they're still producing root stocks.

But when I went there, a lot of the work that was done was by hand. Obviously, there were tractors and there was machinery but they had heavy horses in the nursery because they didn't want to pan the ground - they wanted to keep the ground fluffy for the large number of trees that were produced.

It was really enjoyable. There was a real buzz about the place, until sadly government cuts started coming in and cutting back at all research stations. So, the research station went through a slightly difficult patch then... but it's on the up again now, I'm pleased to say. Staff numbers are still lower, but the work they're doing is still fascinating and really vital for the fruit growing economy and the economy as a whole in horticulture.

When I first went there we had lots of old rural type characters... really, really, lovely men, who had actually come through the war and been on the farm during the war and on other farms during the war, and they had some fascinating anecdotes... They could work all day without any seeming tiredness - and hoeing all day - us youngsters just couldn't keep up with them.

And they had study courses there for youngsters like me at that stage, so we actually had scientists talking to us about the things that they were doing and the sort of problems they were having with pests and what they were doing with pests. And one of the quite amusing things is that entomologists working on particular types of insects... you would find that they started looking a bit like the insects themselves. A bit like people looking like their dogs! But they were very kind and would spend hours quite happily talking to you about their chosen subject.

It was like its own community… It was like living in a little village, really. Everybody knew each other and everybody got on well. The then director, Dr. Tubbs, encouraged that feeling. He was very much in charge of the place and if anybody was ill he made sure that they got sent a bunch of flowers, or somebody went round to visit, or there was help and assistance given. And there were a lot of staff. The agricultural and horticulture staff lived on site then… that's not so much the case now, but yes, it really was a living and thriving community.

Registered charity, 'The East Malling Trust' is the owner of the Research Station and adjacent 'Bradbourne House', which is a Queen Anne Grade I listed house set in parkland. Bradbourne house was built between 1712 and 1715 and was in the ownership of the Twisden family for around 400 years. It was purchased by the Trust in 1938.

Greenways, Addington

David Cameron

In 1978, I went to a function at Greenways and the food was cold and of poor quality and I said to an acquaintance that, "I could do something with this place". So the owner asked to see me. He lived in Jersey – George Fenner – and we did a deal… and I took over the place - bought the place from him.

And I had a large mortgage, needless to say at that time.

Did very well at Greenways… had lots of top quality entertainment - the Drifters, the Nolan Sisters, Acker Bilk, Kenny Ball and his Jazz Band - all kinds of top entertainers there. And I also built 24 bedrooms there, to add a hotel complex to the side of it…

And, in 1982, a programme on television

said the insulation material I was using caused cancer…. there was no truth in it… business more or less collapsed. A year later, I got the apology from the BBC and ITN, but it was too late then, I was broke. I lost my company (Megafoam) and I lost Greenways, as well. It was like a pack of cards all coming down.

Function at 'Greenways'

The site where the 'Greenways' entertainment complex stood lay in Offham parish until boundary changes brought it into Addington in 1985. 'Greenways' was built during the 1930's as an entertainment hall, but the Ordnance Survey Map of 1938 shows that it had already expanded to two main buildings and a popular open air swimming pool. The venue was greatly used by local people in the days before the Local Authority run Larkfield Leisure Centre was built. There were weekly dances and entertainments. After David Cameron took over he added further halls and meeting rooms and, as he says, a hotel complex with 24 bedrooms. After 'Greenways' closed the site stood empty for some years. In the mid-1980s there was a fire there and then, in the early 1990's, the whole complex – hotel, entertainment halls and swimming pool – was demolished. A development of 32 family homes called The Links was built on the site, around a communal green.

LOCAL BUSINESSES AND EMPLOYMENT

Mereworth Shops

Marion Regan and Alison Lowe

Alison: I don't remember really shopping for food of any sort in towns at all in those days. And there were certainly no supermarkets. But we got all we needed in the village and grew other vegetables... And there was George Clark in the garage - he was a great character! If you wanted to know what was going on in the village, you just went and got some petrol from George and heard the latest!

Marion: And, Mrs. Clark... Sylvia - she had a toy shop. And I think they only opened it over Christmas time. I just remember going certain times of the year, and she would open it up for you.

Busbridge's Paper Mill, East Malling

Leslie Fox

My Dad was the foreman in the salle at the mill and finished up (being) the last man in the paper mill. He had to pack up all the existing paper stock and he used to wrap up all the reams of paper. He had to count every sheet and make sure there were no marks in them before he packed them. He packed them up in huge packs with brown sticky paper.

I remember there were four men working in the mill there in the evenings, when I used to take his dinner. There was Mr Hernden, Mr Essey and I think a Mr Day - they all worked 'til 9 o'clock at night.

Mr.Hernden used to operate the guillotine. I was interested in watching them using that - looked a dangerous instrument! I used to walk up through the yard and all these old white paper suds were bubbling away in a huge tank in the mill there.

Papermaking played an important role in the economy of the Maidstone area from the seventeenth century through to the late-twentieth century. There have been, at various times, more than 30 paper mills at work in the immediate area of Maidstone. This was due, mainly, to the number of watermills in this region, in conjunction with the excellent quality of the water provided by the chalk aquifers of the North Downs. Also important was the proximity to ports and towns for the supply of raw materials in the form of rags and cordage etc.; and the proximity to London for the final market place. The arrival of steam power, and paper-making machines, changed matters dramatically in the nineteenth century, with the establishment of paper mills throughout virtually the whole country, and a corresponding collapse in the number of small water-powered paper mills. The twentieth century saw the construction of several large paper mills in North Kent, especially on the south bank of the river Thames. This allowed the use of large ships to bring in the high tonnages of woodpulp, coal, and clay that these modern mills required. In a similar way, the first phase of Aylesford Paper Mills was built in New Hythe, in 1922, on the west bank of the river Medway. Snodland paper mill already existed at this time, having developed from a water-powered corn mill that had been converted to papermaking by about 1740.

A few miles away from the nearest navigable waterway were the East Malling paper mills, on the East Malling stream. One of the three original mills had shut by the middle of the nineteenth century, but the two remaining ones went on to become one important rural paper mill. These two operated independently until about 1850, when they came under the control of George Frederick Busbridge, albeit with him in partnership with different partners at various times. In 1865, the company name became G F Busbridge & Co, and this title changed very little until the business was bought by Wiggins Teape, who closed down the papermaking operation in about 1932. Upper mill, on the south side of Mill Street, had been a self-contained paper mill, with its own papermaking machine and drying loft. Most of the building complex was demolished sometime after 1918, but one or two of the buildings were kept for the cleaning and preparation of the rags that were then turned into paper at Middle mill, on the north side of Mill Street. After all papermaking activity had ceased, Goldwell Farms Ltd took over Middle mill for the production of cider and perry.

by Michael Fuller

Patients, Leybourne Grange Hospital
Valerie Valvassura

At that time, the Leybourne Grange was a working hospital. It had, I think, around a thousand residents. They had villas and some of the patients would be seen locally, because they worked around the area. My neighbour had somebody who used to come to do the garden. The staff would come and see what the job was and they'd assess somebody to see if they were capable of carrying out the work. The patients were in the hospital for many reasons. There were ladies there because they'd become pregnant out of wedlock, which was regarded as wrong in those days, poor souls. I had a lady at my luncheon club who had spent many years in Leybourne Grange because she'd had a baby. It was quite cruel...

On Sundays my family and I would see groups of them walk past the house in order to go to West Malling. There used to be a place called 'The Green Lantern' in West Malling, which was an afternoon tea shop and the patients would be taken out to tea and then return to the hospital.

The grounds of Leybourne Grange were open to walkers and each year they held a fete, where the local youth band used to go and entertain.

'The Grange', originally known as 'Leybourne Grange Colony for Mental Defectives', was set behind gates in spacious grounds of around 270 acres. It was open from 1936 until 1996 and housed 1200 patients. The site of the Leybourne Grange Hospital is currently being developed for housing.

Reeds and Cobdown Sports Day
Linda Javens

At the time when I was at work for Reeds, which was a paper making industry and box making company - anything to do with paper products...

My grandfather had been on the first paper making machine, my dad went there from school and he was in the engineering side - at the box factory, they called it. And then when I left school, I went there. It was almost a follow on, which was nice...

But Reeds was the most wonderful company to work for. The opportunities they gave people... They did give further education 'til eighteen and you could change your job. There was every opportunity in all spheres, there.

And every year they used to put on Cobdown Sports Day. Now that really was wonderful and I used to get involved in that. And we used to have to dress up in country costumes so that we were on the stalls and they were managing the sports... it was really loved by everyone. Unfortunately, if I remember rightly, that had to be closed because the polio epidemic at the time caused a lot of problems. They tried not to let people get in a mass of crowds because polio was pretty bad.

Linda Javens at Reeds and Cobdown Sports Day

Reed's papermaking and conversion operations at New Hythe were conducted on a huge scale, with several independent companies involved. About 8,000 men and women were employed there at the peak of the activities in the 1980s. Aylesford Paper Mills, the papermaking division of Reed's, had a total of 13 papermaking machines at work at various times. Aylesford Newsprint currently operates a fourteenth machine. Reed Corrugated Cases converted some of the mill's papers into countless types of corrugated boxes and cases. In a similar way, Brookgate Industries converted suitable papers into a wide range of coated, creped, impregnated, and laminated papers and boards. Reed Medway Sacks converted sack kraft from Aylesford Paper Mills into numerous types of bags and sacks. Key Terrain manufactured pitch fibre piping systems, and L & P Plastics produced a range of moulded plastic fittings for domestic and commercial drainage systems. Kimberly Clark occupied part of the site, where they produced a range of domestic tissue paper products under the Kleenex mark. Reed's tube factory manufactured millions of paper tubes, which were needed at the centres of all the reels and rolls of paper at the various stages of their conversion.

A considerable infrastructure was needed to support all this activity. This included canteens, a medical centre, a training school, a large R & D facility, a steam and power department, a transport fleet (Reed Transport), a hairdressing service, a banking service, a fire brigade, and many other operations and facilities not included here. Internal transport included a standard gauge railway and several miles of track. Motive power consisted of a group of small steam locomotives, named after famous admirals (Anson, Howe, Nelson, Rodney), and a diesel locomotive (Hornblower).

by Michael Fuller

Polio was a viral disease, a summer plague that usually stopped with the frost. As it was very infectious, public events, cinemas and swimming pools were closed during the outbreak. It left many people paralysed. Patients with paralyses of breathing muscles were confined to an iron lung to help them breathe. Immunisation was introduced in the mid-sixties and this led to eradication of the disease.

Shops, East Malling
Leslie Fox

There was the Reverend Hamilton in the church - we used to go about 6 o'clock Sunday evening as far as I can remember.

There were a number of bakeries in East Malling... There was 'Symonds' in the High Street, and 'Newmans', and also Mr Standing's in Mill Street.

There was a little sweet shop near 'The Rising Sun' or next to 'The Rising Sun' - my parent's lived next door to that for a while. Mr Standing looked after the shop - and his wife and daughter. Plenty of shops... 'Dimberlins' on the corner - big store! - kettles and saucepans and all the old necessaries and groceries. There was 'Jenners' shop in the High Street, with a post office and telephone outside.

There was a sweet shop the other side of the railway bridge - all the kiddies could go in and get their sweets on the way to school - I used to go in there.

There was a hairdresser in a hut opposite the post office in the High Street.

Butchers... as I remember was Mr Chapman.

And there was probably about three dairies. There was Wiggin's and Mr Butler's dairy in Blacklands and all the cows were in the field by the dairy behind Mill Street. There was 'Coleville's Dairy' in the High Street next to the school. And there was Mr Tetherston's Dairy halfway up the Wateringbury Road there in East Malling, just above the High Street.

Symonds Bakery

The Raymar Cinema

Mrs M. A. West

The cinema was situated in Norman Road, just past the cricket meadow. (It is now the site of six/eight houses).

It started life as a NAAFI hut on the grounds of Dover Castle, just after the 1st World War - these things were being sold off. West Malling started a 'hut week' and some furious fund raising went on, and the Dover NAAFI, was relocated to West Malling. Freda Barton took photographs. It was renamed "The Badminton Hall" and all sorts of jollifications went on.

Dances every week according to the 'old locals'. Some quite prodigious bands came i.e. Roy Fox, Harry Roy, etc. Presumably they also played badminton. There was in the 20's and 30's an operatic society - Gilbert and Sullivan etc.

I know they had dances there all the time in the 1939-45 years.

In the early 50's it was sold to Mr and Mrs Halke - strangely enough from Dover. And they turned it into "The Raymar Cinema" and very successful it was to.

In the early 70's, one Christmas, it was the only cinema in Kent to be showing a proper Christmas film. The result was unbelievable. Norman Road was in chaos... coaches, cars, masses of people - from Dartford, Bexley Heath, Herne Bay, Margate, - in fact it looked like the whole of Kent came to stuff themselves in The

Raymar. The locals didn't stand a chance and frankly, neither did they. The capacity was about a hundred.

The Raymar was sadly missed when it closed.

Raymar Cinema

PUBLIC LIFE

A Death at Malling Rural District Council

Mrs M. A. West

There were at least three of us on (shift) and I walked up the road with our shorthand typist who was a large lady who used to smoke Balkinson Brownies. As we got almost to the door she said to me, "If that idiot…" speaking about the caretaker, "…opens that door and says ba ba, ba ba, ba ba,…" she said, "I shall give him a knuckle sandwich."

Well, as we got to the gate of Elmwood House and went in, Jack Brimsted, who was another clerk with us, he came through the church gardens and waved and we went in. Well, the caretaker never said a word - he just opened the door to us.

We went down to our office, which was at the other end, we put the kettle on and we were working away when all of a sudden Vera Maxted said to me, "Where's Brimmy?" I said, "God knows. It's been about half an hour." I was just about to go out and Wook for him when he came in… "Don't you know what happened?" and we said, "No, we don't know what happened." He said, "Surely you knew?" and I said, "What?" He said, "When I got there, just the same time as Colin Hall came in, Roberts (the caretaker) was lying on the floor and he was dead!"

Of course this isn't funny, I know, but the only thing in the way of first aid equipment we had was a couple of old stretchers left over from the isolation hospital which had been up in the woods. Of course they popped Roberts with his coat on on it and they got the doctor out… The mortuary was around the back of 'Forsters' over the other side of the road.

> The isolation hospital, otherwise known as the Hospital for Infectious Diseases, was located in East Malling and is shown on maps from the 1890s to the 1930s. The building is believed to have survived until the 1950s, when it was demolished to make way for a new housing estate.
>
> 'Balkinson Brownies': Balkan Sobranie cigarettes. Sobranie of London (established 1879) were manufacturers of exotic handmade cigarettes such as 'Oval Turkish' and 'Black Russian'. The company was sold to the Gallaher Group in the 1980s and subsequently to Japan Tobacco.
>
> 'Forsters' – A Georgian house next to the doctors' surgery in the High Street and opposite the Council Offices at 123-125 High Street. The mortuary was in the present car park of the surgery.

Amenities Committee, West Malling

Diane Hart

I became chairman of the Amenities Committee. I was on the steering group that chose the Hope statue on our village green and we had the playing equipment put in because the equipment they had was dire - it really was. So when I became Chairman, they all knew that was my project - to fit out the children's play area with some good, bright, sturdy playing equipment.

> The Amenities Committee is a subcommittee of the Parish Council.

The 'Hope' Statue, West Malling.

A New Borough Council...
John Lander

As a councillor, I was on the steering committee that set up Tonbridge and Malling Borough Council. And I was involved with the appointment of, with others of course, the new chief officers. And I was slightly instrumental in persuading the new council to occupy the former Officers' Mess up at Kings Hill as its Headquarters.

It eventually became the new council chamber which in the first instance saved the new borough the cost of building a purpose-built building – so, hopefully, that saved the rate payers a certain amount of money.

I suppose Kings Hill possibly is more or less the geographical centre of the new borough, and it does make a certain amount of sense, I think.

> The District of Tonbridge and Malling was an amalgamation of Tonbridge Urban District, Malling Rural District and parts of Tonbridge Rural District which started to function as a council in 1974. The council was renamed Tonbridge and Malling Borough Council in 1983 when it received borough status.

Citizens Advice Bureau, West Malling
Mike Rowe

I was involved with the Citizens Advice Bureau for thirty years and that was really as a member of the administration committee. I wasn't an advisor. I was, for quite a few years, Chairman of the trustee board of the Malling Citizen's Advice Bureau in West Malling.

In the end we had to close the Bureau because Tonbridge and Malling Borough Council that funded us couldn't sustain the level of funding that we wanted - and costs were escalating and we could see that we wouldn't be able to continue. So, as a charity, we had to close down - but it was a real shame that we did so because the number

of people who used to come in and use the service, particularly people who got into debt or who were in relationship difficulties. In fact, relationship difficulties often end up with debt problems...

It's a great shame that we couldn't continue it really.

> Mike was awarded an MBE for his services to the Citizens Advice Bureau in 2004.
> The Malling Bureau opened at the Clout Memorial Institute in 1976. After an initial trial period under the supervision of Tonbridge it became a fully-fledged and approved Bureau in its own right in 1984 and a registered charity from 1992. Mike Rowe MBE, JP served on the Management Committee from its inception and was Chairman of the Trustee Board from 2000–2009.

Community, Kings Hill
David Murray

My connection previously with RAF West Malling was, I was in the air cadets... and so in 1967 my first flight in a glider was here at RAF West Malling on a winch launch.

So I couldn't believe it then... all those years later... I ended up looking at a property (here). We came up here to look at Kings Hill... fell in love with the concept of what was being offered at the time...

There was planning to be three separate villages - one was a garden village, which was the initial site that was being developed. There was going to be a golfing village and what they called a heathland village. Certainly the garden village progressed and so when we moved here in 1995, it was really small and nice, and very community based. Everybody seemed to know everybody... and obviously compared with now and the future development of nine hundred and seventy five further houses... ...it's going to make it into an enormous area.

So it's rather gone away from the concept that we initially thought was going to happen here at Kings Hill.

When we moved in initially, I got involved in setting up a Neighbourhood Watch scheme... It was quite easy to monitor, I got lots of volunteers - as I said, quite a good community spirit, "Oh, I will be a coordinator in this road" and "I'll be a coordinator" ... so I had about twenty to twenty-five coordinators in the all the roads in this area. We produced a newsletter, called 'Watch It' ...and it was manageable.

A few of us got together and put together a Residents Association. The Residents Association organised social things... we did a picnic on the green, I ended up being Father Christmas at Christmas and we did carols on the green and so, for a few years, we had quite a good social thing going... ...Then there came a point that it was suggested that there should be a Parish Council. I think that started in 1999. So that was four or five years after that we'd moved here. Some of the people that were part of the Residents Association, myself included, put themself up for being elected for the Parish Council.

The Parish Council was formed on 1999 with 8 councillors, some from the existing Residents Association.
Since that time the Parish Council has expanded to 12 councillors with sub committees for Finance & HR, Sports (dealing with the Heath Farm sports complex), Planning and Amenities, as well as the Community Centre Committee. Staffing has increased from a Clerk, to having an assistant clerk, administrative support, two caretakers, cleaning and bar staff as well as a Community Centre Manager, all of which are needed to support an expanding Parish and a thriving Community Centre. The Parish Council has also built an extension to facilitate a privately run nursery and a youth facility, both of which are well attended.

Malling Rural District Council
Mrs M. A. West

Very old-fashioned Malling Rural District Council was ... the people were all vaguely eccentric. I mean, there used to be some extraordinary people come in... There was a fellow there called Bobdog and he had a constant fight in the early 30s with the other rating officer.

And he never would pay until the last possible moment and I know one morning, he came in and he paid his rates, which was about fifteen pounds and he paid it all in ha-pennies. Now, as you know, there was over 200 pennies in the pound and if you think about how many ha'pennies there were in that... and he just poured all these ha'pennies over the counter.

Mrs West worked for Malling Rural District Council from 1952 until 1978.

Decimal coinage was officially introduced in the United Kingdom on 15 February, 1971. This replaced the ancient duodecimal system, with 240 pence to the pound and 12 pence to the shilling (equivalent to 5 new pence). There were 480 'ha-pennies' (half-pennies) to the pound, so 7,200 coins would have been used to pay the rates bill of £15.

Rural District Councils and Parish Councils were created thoughout England and Wales following the Local Government Act of 1894 to introduce elected councils at local and parish level. Malling Rural District Council was replaced by Tonbridge and Malling Borough Council in 1974, created under the Local Government Act of 1972.

New Leybourne Estate
Valerie Valvassura

Prior to the estate being built there was an action group set up to try to prevent them building on the green land at Leybourne - green space is, and was, very precious and so we did fight the development. The Action group took a petition to Downing Street and a lot of people locally supported it. We used to meet and have fundraising projects and events at Leybourne Castle. In those days Colonel and Mrs Harris lived there and they used to let us use the castle. We used to have New Year's Eve parties and various fundraising events throughout the year to raise money to keep the action group going.

Inevitably we failed - and I think that was about 1981 when they cut the first sod, as they say, of the estate. Prior to that it was all farmland and in the middle was a huge house called 'Chimneys', owned by Mr. Pettipiere and his family.... ...and it was all just open farmland everywhere.

Leybourne Castle

The new housing estate at Leybourne was built on the land between Rectory Lane and the A20.

Police, West Malling
Barbara Earl

When I first got posted to West Malling in September 1974, we didn't have personal radios because there was no reception - no signal, and the only radio we had was the force radio in the escort van, or the area car if you were driving that. So once you were out of the car, you were on your own, and we very rarely were doubled up, you know, two officers in one car.

West Malling Police Station was newly built and opened in 1866 following the establishment of the Kent County Constabulary in 1857. The original building included a magistrates' court, which was transferred to a new building behind the Police Station in 1962. The Police Station and Courthouse closed in 1998 and the whole site was eventually sold for redevelopment. The residential development, Victoria Place and Victoria Court, was completed between 2008-2009 and incorporated a small part of the original Police Station.

The Magistracy, West Malling
Mike Rowe

I was, for thirty years, a magistrate and I started in 1981 at the courthouse in West Malling, which was down Police Station Road. Then, there must have been about forty magistrates there - and I joined as a new magistrate... and in those days you didn't put yourself forward... Somebody came to me one New Year's Day and said, "How would you like to be nominated to be a magistrate?" I'd never even thought about it before and I said, "Oh that sounds interesting. What do I have to do?" They said, "Well you have to fill in an application form and then two or three people will come and interview you in your house" - which they did. Three people turned up and interviewed me about my outlook in life and my background and what I thought about the law and then I was appointed.

We used to meet in the Courthouse in West Malling. Over the years it gradually changed because, first of all, they closed the Courthouse in West Malling - it's now, in fact, been demolished and it's a housing estate... and we joined with Maidstone Court and then we joined with several other courts and in the end there were three hundred magistrates all on the one bench.

And when I first started being a magistrate most of what we dealt with was motoring offences, speeding, not having insurance and all these sort of things - but then fixed penalties came in and the police could administer a fixed penalty without the matter going to court. So, a lot of that was swept aside and we ended up dealing mainly with domestic violence and theft and that sort of thing - but not all that much motoring. Occasionally, if somebody was going to be disqualified from driving we'd deal with them. It was fascinating!

West Malling Courthouse, 1985

West Malling Courthouse closed in December 1998. Mike Rowe was Central Kent Bench Chairman from 2004 to 2007 and retired from the Bench in 2012.

The Role of the Parish Clerk, Addington and Trottiscliffe

Barbara Earl

So I'd already been Clerk to Teston Parish Council....

And they said they were desperate for a Parish Clerk in Addington. So I was interviewed and got the job.

So it was lovely, because we never knew what was going to happen... Still meeting people, dealing with all sorts of problems.

Then Trottiscliffe - they needed a Parish Clerk. So Trottiscliffe interviewed me and I got the job.

But because there were two sandpits that affected both parishes - each parish had different views.

So I couldn't tell one parish what the other one was saying. And I used to have to write letters to myself...

So from Trottiscliffe from me as Clerk to Trottiscliffe... To me as Clerk to Addington... Total discretion!!

Barbara was appointed Clerk to Addington Parish Council in May 1980. She eventually served four parishes – Teston, Addington, Trottiscliffe and Wouldham (not all together – though briefly she was responsible for three!)

West Malling Farmers Market

Trudy Dean

About 12 years ago, we didn't feel that the market properly reflected the ethos of a farmers market. It was degenerating into something that was much more arts, crafts and tat basically. As a result, the numbers of people coming were going down and the number of stalls coming was decreasing.

We decided that we wanted to revitalise it and we spotted the government scheme, which I think at that time was called 'Rural Market Towns Scheme'. The government had rightly thought that too many rural market towns were becoming places for estate agents and antique shops and were ceasing to be real places. I heard about it purely by chance at a fire authority meeting of all things, and they were talking through the scheme and put up the names of the towns.

I was all ready to protest and say, "Why isn't West Malling on this list?" and all of a sudden, there it was - it was on the list. But nobody had told West Malling that it was on list! And we only had a very short space of time within which to get a bid in. So we decided that the nucleus of what we wanted to do was the farmers market.

And almost before the contract was signed on the creation of the partnership - we called ourselves 'Malling Action Partnership', the market operator of the farmers market - our jewel in the crown - our central project - went into receivership.

The Borough Council to our disappointment decided to use that as the time when they withdrew their funding... completely. So we all got very cross about it and tried to persuade the Borough Council but they were not for turning. So, in essence, I went to the County Council and said, "This is a nonsense... we have a beautiful town, we have a beautiful medieval market, we have the wish and the ability to redevelop what's a proper farmers market - ticks all the boxes as far as the County Council's job creation schemes are concerned. Please, would you like to give us the money to run the market for a couple of years while we get it back on track?"

And Mr. Carter, who was then, and still is, the County Council's leader, said, "Yes fine, we'll do that!" And we agreed a match funding. So we used fifty percent of the County Council's money and fifty percent from the government grant and I think I'm right in saying that, with a newly appointed company – 'Meopham Farmers Markets', some investment in advertising and a lot of work spreading the word, two months before the end of the two years, the market returned to a level of self-funding, and it's still flourishing now, twelve years later...

The right to hold Saturday markets was granted to the Abbess of Malling by Henry I in 1105, and markets were probably always held in the wide High Street. Grants for markets on Tuesdays and Wednesdays were also given or claimed during the following two centuries, but the Saturday market and three annual cattle fairs were the main events to survive into the post-medieval period. During the eighteenth century the Saturday market declined in popularity and was eventually discontinued, the market house (located opposite the George Inn, by the entrance to West Street) being removed by popular demand in 1747. An attempt to revive the Saturday market in the 19th century failed (recorded as "little frequented" in 1839), though the fairs continued in popularity into the 20th century.

West Malling Farmers' Market.

West Malling Police Station

Barbara Earl

There was one of the rural PC's... quite chummy he was with an egg farmer. So we always had plenty of eggs and people used to come and buy their eggs.

The best bit was Christmas... another of the rural PC's was in with one of the turkey farmers. So you used to put your order in about October... roughly what size turkey you wanted - of course they were still being fattened up. And then they were all slaughtered and there used to be like a working party, plucking the chickens!

SIGNIFICANT PEOPLE AND VISITORS

Alan Skinner, Trottiscliffe

Mike Towler

The ring leader in the village ... I suppose you could have called him, was our local farmer who was the most superb man. Tragically, he died far too young...

To give you an idea of his popularity, you couldn't get into the church for the funeral - there was a great crowd outside. He was superb! He was involved with the Parish Council. In fact, he was involved with everything and anything that went on in this village - he loved the village. I've never heard a single critical comment against him. In fact, if you look opposite the pond outside Miller's Farm, which is where he was ... there's a village sign ... and if you get out and peer at the post very closely, you'll see that there is a notice on there, telling you that it was erected in his memory. And we didn't have a village sign before that ... that was done in memory of Alan Skinner.

Alan Skinner (1920-1983) was brought up on his father's farm in Trottiscliffe. During the war, as a farmer's son, he was in a reserved occupation and remained at Miller's Farm. Thus, he met his wife, Jean (d. 2012) in 1941. As 21 year old Jean Shoebridge, she came from her home in Bromley to work as a land-girl on nearby Court Lodge Farm. The couple married in 1947. The family were at first concerned that Jean would not fit in, as she was a 'townie'. However, they grew to love her and she became the archetypical farmer's wife and countrywoman. Like her husband, she gave long and faithful service to Trottiscliffe.

Trottiscliffe Village Sign

A Life of Service – Jesse Smith, Mereworth

Dave Smith

My father, Albert Jesse Smith - 'Jess', as he soon became affectionately known, started his career working at the Village Store in Mereworth. Jess learned to drive before the days when driving licences were required and took over the daily deliveries of groceries, newspapers, alcoholic drinks and fuel oils such as paraffin, turpentine and methylated spirit. Every day the van would be loaded up in the morning for the "round" for that day. These extended over many miles - from Mereworth covering Wateringbury and Teston to the east, East Peckham to the south, Hadlow and West Peckham to the west and also West Malling and East Malling to the north.

My father actually did much more than just deliver the groceries. He would frequently collect and deliver the pensions for those who were unable to get to the Post Office. He would also always carefully scrutinise all the orders as they were made up and would often spot things which he was sure that the housewife had forgotten. He would put these extra items in as well and if his supposition was correct, as it usually was, he would add these to the bill.

Going on rounds with my father meant, of course, that I also got to know many of the customers well. There were often humorous situations, such as the lady who always ordered "Kit-e-Kat". When he asked, on one occasion, why he had never seen her cats, my father was told, in confidence, that she had actually picked up a tin by mistake several years earlier and, when opened, it was mistaken for fish paste. Her husband liked it so much that she continued to use it when making his packed lunch sandwiches - obviously he was not aware of the real nature of the filling.

The shop was taken over again around the late 40s/early 50s by Mr McConnell. Towards the end of the 1950s Mr McConnell retired and the shop entered a difficult period during which several new owners came and went. First, was Mr Brooks who ran it successfully for a few years but, again, then decided to retire. Next came Mr Riches, who had spent most of his life in South Africa. He had absolutely no experience of running such a business and soon sold it on – he is not even recorded in the electoral rolls of the period. Mr Westerall was the next owner. He too had spent most of his life abroad in South America and had an extremely attractive Mexican wife, which I think caused a bit of a stir in the community at first. Nevertheless, after a few years the business was sold on again - to Mr Burns.

In my final year at university in London, Mr Burns was obviously finding the financial situation very challenging and spoke to my father about this. Carefully and considerately ascertaining that I would be soon finishing at university and starting a job, he postponed the inevitable decision to make my father redundant. Nevertheless, when the decision finally came in about 1965 it was a devastating shock for my father who was only 58. After less than a year he found a job at the ironmongers in West Malling, working in the shop and also delivering and collecting stock. He was soon back to his normal self, but during the next two years a succession of medical problems surfaced. It was a tremendous shock to me when he died at the age of 61. Tributes to my father kept arriving in the post for several weeks after his death.

Delivery Bikes outside Mr. Gould's Shop, 1935

The Village Stores in Mereworth was situated on the bend close to the church between the "Black Lion" and "Torrington" public houses and, at the time that Jess started work there in 1920, it was owned by Mr Warren. The son of this proprietor became well known later as the author of "A Boy In Kent", which was set in Mereworth and drew heavily on the local inhabitants of the village for its characters.

During the following years the store was taken over by Mr Wyeth and then, perhaps temporarily, by Mr Broad, before finally being bought by Mr Gould.

Dave has a copy of an undated document produced by Mr Gould emphasising that he was retaining the services of Jess to ensure that the customers' interests continued to be safeguarded – a document that his parents treasured.

'A Boy in Kent' written by C. Henry Warren, recalling the countryside of the author's childhood, was first published in 1937.

SIGNIFICANT PEOPLE AND VISITORS

Community, Church and a Royal Visitor, Addington

Sylvia Butler

My parents were very involved in the community. My mother belonged to the Mothers Union and the Women's Institute attending all their activities. My father, Alfred Baker, helped Fred Martin with stalls at the annual fete. He also worked part time as a gardener for Miss Norah Hardy. He attended various events - whist drives etc., held in the old village hall.

I was christened, confirmed and married in Addington church, as was my mother. My daughter Sandra was also christened and married there.

I joined the choir when I was eight and, after choir practice on a Thursday night, we played table tennis and billiards during the winter and, in the summer, we played cricket and rounders on a piece of land in Park Road.

My brother Denys and I were in the church choir for many years.

Princess Margaret attended our church quite frequently with her equerry Lord Plunket. He lived at the Mount Offham, where she used to stay. As she sat in the front pew, I had a clear view of her from the choir stalls. She was quite a fidget which surprised me, as we were taught to sit still.

I think it was the only time the church was full!

The Royal Family were friends with Patrick, 7th Baron Plunket, (1923-1975) who lived with his aunt, The Hon. Mrs. Rhodes, (also d. 1975) at the Mount, Teston Road, then in Addington, but now in Offham.

Lord Plunket was an equerry to King George VI and then to the young Queen Elizabeth. He acquired the Coronation Oak for the village which is now a splendid specimen in the churchyard. It grew as a sapling in Windsor Park. The family always attended church when staying in the village and came to at least one of the fêtes at The Vale. Jack Gower, who ran a shop on Clearway, recalls Lord Plunket coming in to buy fruit for the Queen Mother, who gently acknowledged Jack's best choice of apple with a smile and wave from the car. Mrs Rhodes ran a Sunday School for the children of Clearway, and it is told that the children lined up on the drive to the Mount and curtsied when Princess Margaret or others in her family came back from church. Lord Plunket, who did not marry, is buried in the Royal Family's private burial ground at Frogmore, Windsor Park.

Cricket and the Village Fete, Mereworth

Ann Fisher

I remember the original cricket pavilion... I don't remember my father playing cricket but he did, apparently - he played for the village. But I remember because there used to be the annual pub cricket match between West Peckham and Mereworth and my husband used to play. And I used to do the teas in the old Cricket Pavilion - and when you think... there wasn't running water, there wasn't a flush toilet, it was just so basic. And we were quite fortunate that the castle changed hands and it was an Arab gentleman that bought it. And, through fund raising in the village and a great contribution from him, we are able to have now what is the sports pavilion - which was a great step forward for the cricket and football teams and general use of the village...

The Arab gentleman who generously underwrote the cost of the sports pavilion and was the owner of Mereworth Castle at that time, was His Excellency the Arab Emirates Ambassador to the United Kingdom, Mahdi Al Tajir.

Doctor Who at Addington Quarry

Joan Bygrave

The quarry was interesting in itself, because it was like a vast moonscape and I've actually got a photograph of when they photographed some of the early series of 'Doctor Who' down there. My children first learned about trompe l'oeil... The Tardis was a model that stood on a sand covered table in the distance. And the Daleks were, of course, just mechanical things. I've got a photograph in which the Daleks are all lined up with their jackets around them to keep the sand from blowing into the mechanics, and way in the distance you can see this little tiny model standing on the table.

Dr. Who at the Addington Sand Quarry

The first Doctor Who series was screened in 1963 and was filmed at Addington later that decade.

Gilbert and Sullivan Operas in West Malling in the 60s.

Linda Javens

One really good thing that happened in West Malling in the mid 60's...

We had four sisters called the 'Collins Sisters'. They'd been semi-professional musically wise - very clever girls they were! And they lived in 'Lavenders', which is now a residential home. They decided, having met my mum, who was a pianist, that they would like to put on through the WI, Gilbert and Sullivan operas, which we did every year. Mum was the pianist, Dad played the drums, I was in it singing, my sister was singing and my sister-in-law and all local people.... and we had a wonderful time. That also raised funds, I believe, towards the Village Hall. So that was really quite a venture... They were very well loved in the area.

The Collins Sisters with Fred and Margaret Gandon (in pink)

Graham Sutherland and Trottiscliffe Cricket Club

Louis Fissenden

Now, when we first moved to the idea of starting the Cricket Club in Trottiscliffe up - because there was one pre-war... The Osmer boys... (they had a farm in Trottiscliffe) - we all got together and formed it - well they did, I didn't - I just joined.

Anyway, money was tight. Graham Sutherland said to me, "I'll design you some colours", and they turned it down because one or two of them had bought caps and they couldn't afford to buy another cap. And I told them it was a mistake at the time!

Now, of course eventually he (Graham Sutherland) started to become famous and he spent all his life in Menton after that... Mind you, he's in the churchyard at Trottiscliffe.

And Reg White lived next door to 'The George'. He was another President – 'Reg Mineral Waters'. He was the Chairman of

the Parish Council and Malling (Rural District) Council. You need all these people in certain places - which a lot of people don't really understand. It's not what you know... it's who you know!

Trottiscliffe Cricket Club started after the war, and Lou Fissenden, who was then living in that village, was one of its first members. Their ground was Key's Croft, a piece of land next to Trottiscliffe School. The land had been donated for the benefit of the village by the long serving Rector, Canon Frederick Fremlin Key (d. 1957, buried at Trottiscliffe), and was named after him. Lou recalls that the club had to gain permission to use the ground each year from Malling Rural District Council (the Parish Council now owns the land as the recreation ground, but had not yet then come into being).

The renowned artist Graham Sutherland (1903-1980) owned The White House, which faces the small green and the George Public House in the centre of Trottiscliffe. From 1947 to the 1960's, much of his work was inspired by the time he spent in the South of France. He purchased a property at Menton in 1955, and spent little time at Trottiscliffe, but asked to be buried in the churchyard. Trottiscliffe church, whose very ancient origins are confirmed by its double dedication (to St. Peter and St. Paul), nestles under the scarp of the North Downs. It was traditionally in the patronage of the Bishop of Rochester, who had a summer 'palace' next door to the church (now a private house). The pulpit in Trottiscliffe Church is from Westminster Abbey. The parish is part of BART United Benefice.

"Reg Mineral Waters" got his nickname from his business, which owned the famous brand of R. White's Lemonade. Robert and Mary White began selling lemonade in 1845, in Camberwell, London. R. White & Sons Ltd. was incorporated as early as 1894. Whitbreads bought the company in the 1960's and later sold the brand to the Britvic Corporation. The brand thrived and during the 1970's also included orangeade, cream soda, etc. The lemonade still contains real lem ons. (from Wikipedia)

One of Trottiscliffe Cricket Club's last fixtures took place on 28 September 1958, at Key's Croft, against the newly founded Addington Village Cricket Club (see 'Cricket and Drama in Addington by Margaret Castle). It closed at the start of the 1960's, through lack of active members. However, at the time of the Millennium, a 'one-off' Ladies Cricket Club was formed which won a local competition run in celebration of the event.

People of Mereworth

Ena Wickens

On Sundays there was Sunday school, and then Sunday afternoons there was a children's service at St Lawrence's church. We were

given a book and each time we attended, we were given a stamp depicting things from the bible. We sometimes attended the evening service and we were also in the choir. We got paid halfpenny for Friday night practice and one penny for Sunday service.

The Reverend H.B. Mayne was the rector. He was an ex naval man. I have seen him sitting in a bosun's chair and painting the faces of the church clocks. He also played cricket for the Mereworth club.

Mr Tapping was headmaster at the Mereworth School and then Miss Vennell in my school days.

I can remember the owners of Yotes Court, Mr and Mrs Woodall, holding a big firework display in the park and we also were given a lovely tea. Mr Harmswoth (who later became Lord Rothermere) owned Mereworth Castle. He gave all the children of Mereworth School a lovely Christmas party which was held in the school. The partition that divided two classrooms was pushed back and the Christmas tree was as tall as the room. Every child had the most lovely present and there was loads of food and every child had a goodie bag to take home.

My father was in the Royal Horse Artillery in the 1914-1918 war. When they came back home from France he bought the French flag with him and, for years, it stood on the right side of the altar in St Lawrence's Church. The Union Jack was on the opposite side.

At the village hall there used to be a working men's club. Mr Henry Moon was steward, then after him my father took on the role. The W.I. had their meetings there. There were also dances held, organised by Mrs Bessie Waterman. The welfare was held there, that was where the mums used to take the children, from babies up until they went to school, to be weighed. Miss Champion ran the welfare.

The Girls Friendly Society (GFS) was also held there and I remember the Reverend Mr Mayne used to take us on the Rectory lake in his boat.

I worked at the grocers at the crossroads until I had my daughter, Ann. It was owned by Mr W. S. Gould. When the hop pickers were down from London he used to put a barricade across the door and they had to queue up outside to be served.

The petrol station in the street was owned by Mr Boorman - he was called 'Blacky Boorman'. There was just one petrol pump in those days. The bulk of his work seemed to be repairing cycles and mending punctures. He used to work until midnight. And sometimes, after doing repairs, he sold paraffin. You would often see him on his old cycle, which had a rack on the front, delivering paraffin to his customers. The shop was taken over by his daughter and son-in-law, Mrs Sylvia and Mr George Clark, and they ran it until they retired.

Next door to the garage was a shop which was once a butcher's, run by Mr Drake. It then went on to be a shoe repairers, also run by My Drake.

Mr James, who was the local policeman,

Mr. Hook, Mr. Boorman and Mr. Watts at Mereworth Garage

was a good artist. He did a pencil sketch of the church. It was given to the fete to be put in the draw. My older brother was lucky enough to win it. My sister lives in Norfolk and she now has it hanging in her house.

In Kent Street, on the stretch between Butchers Lane and The Malling Road, was the Methodist church - now changed to a house. Mr Bell took the services there and played the harmonium. If you attended so many times, you got a shiny disk. We called them medals. Also, on some occasions, they would hold a magic lantern show. As children we thought this was wonderful.

Mr Wilson (he was called Dusty Wilson by the villagers) was the road sweeper. He had a handcart, broom and shovel and he would go around the village sweeping the roads and tidying the verges.

Mr Long was the carrier. He had a lorry and would travel from the village to Maidstone taking goods to market and bringing goods back. Some of the older boys and girls used to run behind him and jump on the back of the lorry. As you can imagine, the lorry never travelled very fast. The villagers called him Dodger Long.

Royal Visitor, East Malling
Douglas Rabjohn

The Duke of Edinburgh came here many years ago. He wasn't the Duke of Edinburgh then... I think he was just called Prince Philip. He visited the Reeds Paper Mill at the bottom of New Hythe Lane and had his lunch down there. From there he was brought up New Hythe Lane and up to visit the Research Station.

I went down to the bottom gate with my class to wait to see him and give him a cheer when he came up here. The Research Station sent a tractor - a very buffed up tractor and

trailer with a very clean bale of straw down to New Hythe Lane... ...And we were patiently waiting there... the police had closed the road... nothing happened... Then a bit later on, the Duke of Edinburgh appeared sitting on this bale of straw, towed by a tractor, and we gave him a cheer. He wasn't very cheerful at all, he didn't smile or anything... but that was all right because, once he'd gone through the gates about 2 o'clock, I just dismissed the children... they went to their homes and so we got the rest of the afternoon off!

The Beatles, West Malling Airfield
Ann Fisher

Another memory of the airfield is when The Beatles were there filming 'Magical Mystery Tour' and I was about twelve or thirteen and I was allowed to have a couple of days off of school to go to the airfield. And I actually met The Beatles and got the autographs, which I've subsequently sold, but hey! It's memories that can never be taken away from you - at the time it was great!

And when I met who was going to be my husband, he was a big Beatles fan, and he was rather envious that I'd got to meet them and spend a couple days and watch them filming.

'The Magical Mystery Tour' was first shown on television on Boxing Day in 1967.

Local people were used as extras in the film. Community Heritage Panel member, Linda Javens recalls that John Lennon was visiting West Malling one day and he took her Grandad's hat from him and wore it in part of the film.

The way it was in Addington

Joan Scott

There was a Miss Cholmeleys and a Miss Hardys. Miss Hardy lived at 'The Vale' but that's all been knocked down now. They ran the village, actually, you know... they were the ladies of the village in those days ... It was like that in those days.

There were quite a lot of poor people ... and Miss Cholmeley used to knit them jerseys. I remember that!

Addington Vale

The period in time that Joan Scott describes is pre-War. Miss Katherine (d. 1945) and Miss Norah Hardy (d. 1963, aged 87) were born in London but came to the Vale, on East Street, in 1881, aged 5 and 4 respectively. Addington Vale was an ancient building, much altered and extended during the Victorian period. They both gave enormous service to the church and their community. Miss Norah followed her father as organist and Miss Katherine became the sole woman councillor on Malling Rural Council at the end of the 1930's and into the Second World War. After Miss Norah's death the house had no further occupants, and was demolished in 1970. A small development of family homes was built on the site.

Miss May (d. 1952) and Miss Aline Cholmeley (d. 1960) were their near contemporaries. They came to Addington from Easton, in Lincolnshire in 1914, first renting St. Vincents and then buying the property in the 1920's. They were also stalwart supporters of the community and church. As Joan says, they were tremendous knitters, and soldiers during the 2nd World War were well kitted out!

After the sale of the manor in the 1920's, the two groups of sisters, Mrs. Hardy, and her son, Lionel (both d. 1933), took on a dual "squire's family" role in the village. Despite having limited means, both families helped those worse off than themselves. The village fête was held at Addington Vale in the days before the Recreation Ground was established. They funded medical and social care, such as a trip to the seaside for a child to recover from illness, or a cottage hospital bed in the days before the NHS. That is how it was in those days!

THE IMPACT OF WAR

Bombs along the A20

Tony Briggs

What I do remember is my grandfather, he was church organist at Offham and that was his sort of Sunday job - on his bike, he'd cycle off to church. And I remember during the war, he was cycling on the A20, and Jerry* decided that he would drop a string of bombs along the A20. And one fell about 200 yards in front of him, and one fell 200 yards behind him... blew him off his bike... he came out covered in dust after this raid.

*'Jerry' was slang for 'German' during World War II.

Paddlesworth Farm

Trevor Lingham

I have a photograph of the old farm and Queen Anne House, which is still there. It's in a very derelict state at the moment but it's still standing.

Probably ten years before the start of World War Two the house was vacant and empty. During the war there was a training camp for soldiers up on Holly Hill and the army requisitioned the house for practising what they called 'house clearing'. So, as you can understand, it got very beaten up and blown up during the war.

After the war, the department concerned with the government gave the land owners, 'Blue Circle', money to compensate for the damage - to repair the property. But in fact they didn't repair it, they gutted it completely - took out all the internal walls and floors, dropped it

As well as the army camp at Holly Hill there was a large army camp above Trottiscliffe during WWII.
The camp, which occupied an area where part of the public open space is now, included large numbers of Nissan huts and a theatre/cinema as well as training areas.

all down in the cellar and concreted it over, so thus, all it is now is a shell. And with the money they built another farm house, which is there at the moment. The actual house itself is in a very dangerous condition but it's still quite an imposing building when you look at it and hopefully, one day, it will be restored

Paddlesworth Farm

Paddlesworth Farm now resides in Snodland Parish though it was originally a sub manor of Birling. The training camp on Holly Hill is half in Birling and half in Snodland.
After the house was stripped out it was used for a grain store until not suitable for a modern farm. After twenty to twenty five years of supporting weights of 20 to 30 tonnes of grain and the shaking and vibrating from the grain handling equipment, the grand Old House looks in a sad state, though it still retains its composure.

Peace Day Celebrations, West Malling

Tony Briggs

My grandfather was working in the bakehouse doing night work... A load of airmen from the aerodrome marched down with a band made up of anything they could find that made a noise - saucepans, tin cans, anything... and marched down the high street outside here, and my grandfather, apparently said, "What's going on?"

They said, "Peace has been declared." They were the first to hear, obviously, being from the aerodrome.

And so my grandfather said, "Whoopee! Wait

THE IMPACT OF WAR

Tony Briggs (second from left) with family, Peace Day Celebrations 1945

a minute!" and went indoors in the bakehouse and got a bucket of whitewash, which was always in the bakehouse, because health regulations of the day forced us to whitewash the coal hole - what good it did, I don't know!

He got this bucket of whitewash, went to the front, and wrote 'PEACE' right down the front of the road in front of the shop in large letters and they danced all round it. My grandfather had been the church organist and played the piano... he dragged his piano out the front

door into the road and they played all the old war songs and they all sang round his piano in the early hours of the morning. And, of course, we lived next door in number two, and we all woke up and we went out with him and watched them all dancing around the piano and around the 'PEACE'. Funny!

There were never any photographs of it, because that time of day... nobody had cameras as such... but I remember that, as a kid, in 1945. That was quite something actually!

The Battle of Britain

Barbara Harper

I'm probably the only person alive around here that was in the Battle of Britain, or knows anything about it. Not only was I alive then - but I was in it!

It was awful... frightening... noisy... terrifying! It was all going on overhead. Planes were dropping down on the ground and the pilots were... black faces - absolutely burnt...

You can't forget that... it sticks in your mind...

But at least we were doing a useful job - and survived it.

I've got a photograph of me and the 'VAD's' - the 'Voluntary Aid Detachment' it was called. We weren't called up - we volunteered. And I've got a photograph of Leeds Castle with Lady Bailey sitting in the middle. Of course she donated the castle to the Red Cross for the duration of the war...

VAD Hospital, Malling Area

THE IMPACT OF WAR

The War Years 1939-1945

Mrs M. A. West

In one of Noel Cowards' plays (I have never known which one) a languid lady drifts through saying "Nothing's been the same since the elephant died" and that remark can be applied to those six years.

Nothing seemed to happen, and then came Dunkirk... The trains returning were slower, full of wounded men.

I remember I was going to Maidstone, and we came in sight of Preston Hall (Military Hospital) and the conductor said "Oh my God, look", and outside of the hall at the bus stop were four of them.. Uniforms pressed, boots and buttons gleaming, they were smothered in bandages, one on crutches, i.e. walking wounded. "They were going", they said, "to the pictures." They offered their fare to the conductor who just waved them on the bus. He couldn't speak. He wasn't the only one. Everyone was in tears.

It stayed quiet for a few weeks. Mind you, if you sat in the garden you could hear the guns from France and the coast. And then the blitz started.

Battle of Britain Sunday, I remember standing at the top of the steps of our shelter in the orchard and the sky full of enemy aircraft, all in formation to bomb London. About three quarters an hour later they returned, scattered, dropping their bombs willy nilly, just to get rid of them.

I think we had about seven bombs in the orchard. One fell at the bottom of Clare Lane as it bent into Mill Street, the blast going towards the park so no windows were broken.

West Malling fared worse. A time bomb fell in the conservatory of a house on Town Hill. When it eventually exploded it killed the 80 year old parents of Mr Jones, the deputy clerk to Malling Rural District Council - they had refused to leave.

In a subsequent raid, a family was killed in 'Maire's Nest'. The nearby 'George Inn' public house - now replaced by 'Tesco' - was frequented, as they all were, by troops and hop pickers.

The hop pickers also kept the fire brigade busy...

The brigade was manned by volunteers - fellows employed at the paper mills on night shift. And if you were fortunate enough to be standing at the bus stop and the fire warning went - it was always a hopper hut alight - these volunteers would hurtle up on their bicycles, braces flying, shirt scrambled into, rush into the station - three minutes, out came the fire engine, bell clanging madly, chaps with their helmets on, buttoning up tunics. It was a stirring, bustling scene.

If, after the war, you went out for a ride in a car... the hop fields and the hopper huts... the flickering fire light... the scene was medieval... but it took them out of the East End - which was still in ruins.

> 'Maire's Nest' is the name of a row of cottages that had occupied the site that is presently Tesco's car park.

Evidence of the War in Mereworth

Roy Keeler

I remember in about '63, I found a big old beech that was past its prime and was beginning to waver in the breeze, and to my astonishment when we got it on the floor, right in the very top of it, there was part of the wing frame of a Mosquito. And it was just a beech frame, with the aluminum on it.

And there's a lot of bomb holes out there...

The woodland I managed ran up round one side of the airfield and there was a lot of evidence of wartime activity. There's an underground command post up there and goodness knows what else - we found all sorts of stuff.

Quite by accident once I nearly lost a tractor driving through one place and there was a shelter underneath the ground. Everything else was blocked off and there were just these slabs over the top, and one of them broke! But that was all filled in and that's all been sorted out now.

But also, other things I've found spread all over the wood... Every now and then if you were clearing a new ride or something, you'd come across a length of copper cable, and that was where they'd laid cable all over the woods, and then they'd put lights out there to have a fake 'Malling Airfield'. So that got bombed instead of the airfield, which is probably why we've got a fair section of bomb holes!

Woolwich Central School evacuees outside Addington Church, 1939

The Woolwich Boys in Addington

Joan Scott

The Woolwich boys came from London during the war, they were billeted down here, and a lot of people had one or two of the children.

They used to go to Mr Stow who was their Head teacher. He used to take lessons and they had to have them in the village hall as there was nowhere else for them.

The boys that Joan refers to were pupils at Woolwich Central School for Boys. The pupils were aged between 11 and 15. Some boys lived in Addington and others in Wateringbury, where girls from their sister school were billeted. They came with their teachers, and a number lived at the Seekers Trust. Although the mansion had by then been commandeered by the Royal Air Force, the boys ate their meals in the servants' hall. To begin with they shared the small village school, (a half day for each group), but later took their lessons in the Village Hall. They came to church and some boys acted as servers, or helped with pumping the organ – electricity only arrived half way through the war. As teenagers, a number owned bikes, and on occasion would bicycle back to Woolwich on a Friday evening, returning for school by Monday morning. This was not an approved jaunt!
In 1944, when the Germans began to launch V1 and V2 missiles, the school evacuated to the West Country. The group continued to visit Addington for fifty years, hav ing a service at St. Margaret's church on each occasion. As part of their 50th reunion they donated a new Rectors' name board for the church.

Wartime, East Malling
Leslie Fox

In the war I was based in London and I used to try and get home weekends 'cause my mother was on her own.

There was one weekend... there was a plane down, up on the corner of Well Street and Heath Farm. He had landed on the corner of the hop garden.

I went up and had a look and they said the pilot had lost his head... he'd flown, landed the plane under the hop garden wires. His trainee was alright, he got out of the plane and went and reported it at Broadwater Farm, along the road.

It was quite exciting in those days - weekends...

Another weekend there was a bomber over the top. Somebody said it was a Junkers 88 and he'd been firing at the Spitfires who were trying to shoot him down, and they'd shot the engine or something to pieces and he wanted to land at East Malling aerodrome. I think he landed and I believe they fired at him when he landed. I don't know... I was told that they did.

Wartime Memories, Victory and Easter Eggs!
Margaret Ivell, Birling

Dad had to put up blackouts... all the lights had to be blacked, and you weren't allowed to light bonfires after dusk either, because of the light. And, of course, church services were held during the day, because you couldn't have churches lit up either. Stations weren't lit - everything was dark. That's how it was - you didn't think any different.

I remember my dad coming home and throwing this newspaper down and saying to my mother, "It's over!" and I can still see that headline that said "Victory". And I thought we would all get sweets the next day, and everything would come back to normal, when in fact it got worse and worse, didn't it? But yes, I do remember that. I'm sure it was the Daily Mirror - but I just remember those words... "It's over!"

I can remember the first Easter egg I had... And it was in a shop in West Malling and I cycled back home and told my mother about these Easter eggs I'd seen in the shop, and begged and begged and begged her for one, and eventually she gave in and gave me the money and the ration books, and I cycled back and got this Easter egg. And then I came down with tonsillitis and couldn't eat it!

Wartime West Malling
Tony Briggs

We had a static water tank on this green - about 1000 gallons of water in case of bombing.

The other thing I remember about that period was that Abingdon House – the big house opposite - was an Army camp during the war, with soldiers. And every so often, they used to have mock battles in the street here, using blanks, of course. And they'd poke their guns through our fence and us kids used to sit at the window and watch them, and it was better than going to the pictures – it really was... and throwing smoke bombs and all these firecrackers. It was just like being on the front line... and they had a gun on the green as well. I can't remember what sort of gun it was. I think was a Bofor or something of that ilk.

> Abingdon House, No. 9 High Street, is a Grade II listed early 19th-century house. Parish rate records show the occupants as 'Military' between 1940 and 1943.
> The Bofors Anti-Aircraft Gun was introduced in 1934 and used by the British Army throughout World War II.

TRANSPORT

East Malling Roads
Wendy King

There wasn't much in the way of the road that goes through here now called Chapman Way - that was never ever here. And when we moved to Clare Park Estate, all we had at the back of our house was a small lane called Blacklands and that used to go straight through and come out at the bottom of Clare Lane.

The only other roads we had in East Malling were New Road which either joined up with London Road, Larkfield, or went to East Malling village - and there was also Mill Street which led to West Malling...

The houses on the Clare Park estate that Wendy mentions in her story were built in 1951. The area had previously been part of the Clare Park estate that had been owned by the Wigan's and was sold off in lots at an auction on 22nd Oct 1953. The auction was held at the Royal Star Hotel, Maidstone.
The Blacklands track still exists today – it runs from the ragstone, former lodge, gatehouse in New Road, through to Clare Lane and is a public footpath (No 118).

Getting About - West Malling
Linda Javens

Always the area was served with a very, very good bus service – excellent! It didn't matter where you wanted to go in the area, all corners, about every ten minutes, there was a bus. So, it was only just a short step for me to get up to the bus stop. So everywhere I went, was on the bus. I went to school on the bus - both schools on the bus, and then when I went to work, it was down in Aylesford - I went on the bus. Anything I wanted to do socially and quite often it was in Maidstone - we had the pictures, I was a member of the 18 plus group which was a very interesting group and I can remember coming home on the last bus, which probably would get into West Malling about midnight. I didn't have to worry about walking along the road. And we didn't have

telephones, so goodness knows what my mum and dad used to think, but I used to arrive home, can you believe it? I mean, you'd have a fit now if the girls did it!! But it was always on the bus... I didn't learn to drive until my later years, I didn't feel the need.

Getting About - Birling
Margaret Ivell

There weren't as many cars... As I said, when we moved into the Bull Road, there were only three houses with vehicle access. In fact, I couldn't drive a car and I used to cycle from Birling to New Hythe, to Reeds, to work, and back again, in all weathers. It was the only way I could get there! I used to walk from here to the antenatal clinic in Snodland... and walked back again...

Mind you, I did learn to drive eventually!

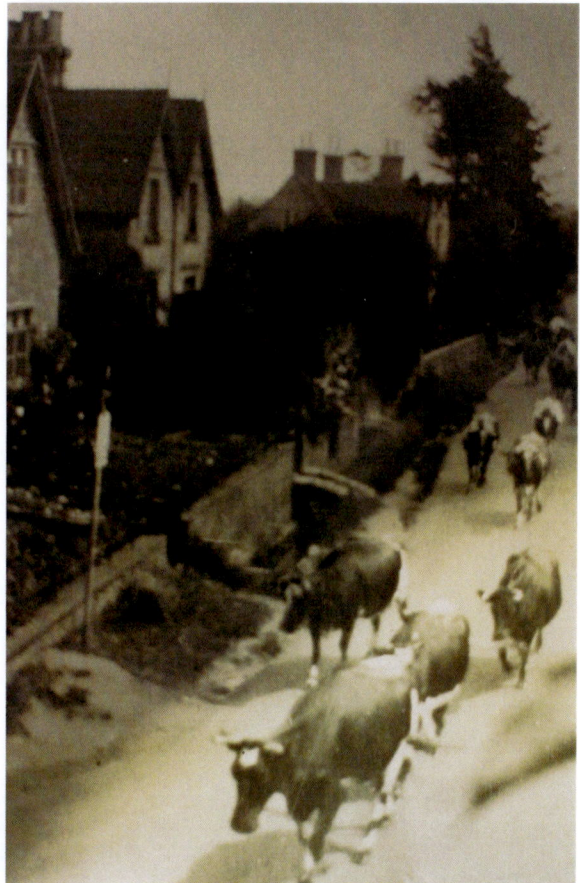

Bull Road, Birling

Railway Station, Offham
Mike Rowe

The railway line came through many years ago, and it used to be a level crossing at the bottom of Teston Road - where it crosses and goes down to the A20. And there used to be a level crossing there, with a crossing keeper, and that closed by act of Parliament in the late 1960s and the road was diverted through what used to be the goods yard. There used to be a platform there and a goods yard, and it now meets the bottom of Seven Mile Lane under the railway bridge. So, in the year 2000, I interviewed a lady who had lived in Offham all her life and she described the early part of the 20th century... A man in the village used to take people down to the railway station in his truck. So, there used to be local transport, but that's now gone – so, it's once again, another thing that's gone with the years gone by.

Offham Level Crossing, 1966

The statutory notice of the road closure that is mentioned in Mike's story, was issued in 1966.

Seven Mile Lane, Mereworth
Marion Regan and Alison Lowe

Alison   Seven Mile Lane, which is rather a busy road now, an absolutely horrible road really - it used to be so peaceful. And one could let children cycle wherever they wish or ride their ponies - both of my daughters had ponies. They didn't have to tell us where they'd gone even. They'd say, "We're going up into the woods", or, "We're going down to see a friend in the village"...

Marion   My grandmother grew up at Barons Place, born in 1900, and she had two sisters who were a little older than her, and she remembers if they heard a car at Mereworth crossroads, they had time to run in from the garden, grab their hats and run along to the end of the road to see if it made it up the hill. So that was the early days of cars...

Alison   ...and if any vehicles got stuck and just couldn't get any further, then a couple of horses from the farm were collected out and hitched up to pull them up the hill.

Marion   Because it's quite a steep...

Alison   And also, these little girls of that period... they not only grabbed their hats... they had time to put on their button boots ...

Marion   Oh yes, their button boots, yes... she told us that...

Seven Mile Lane

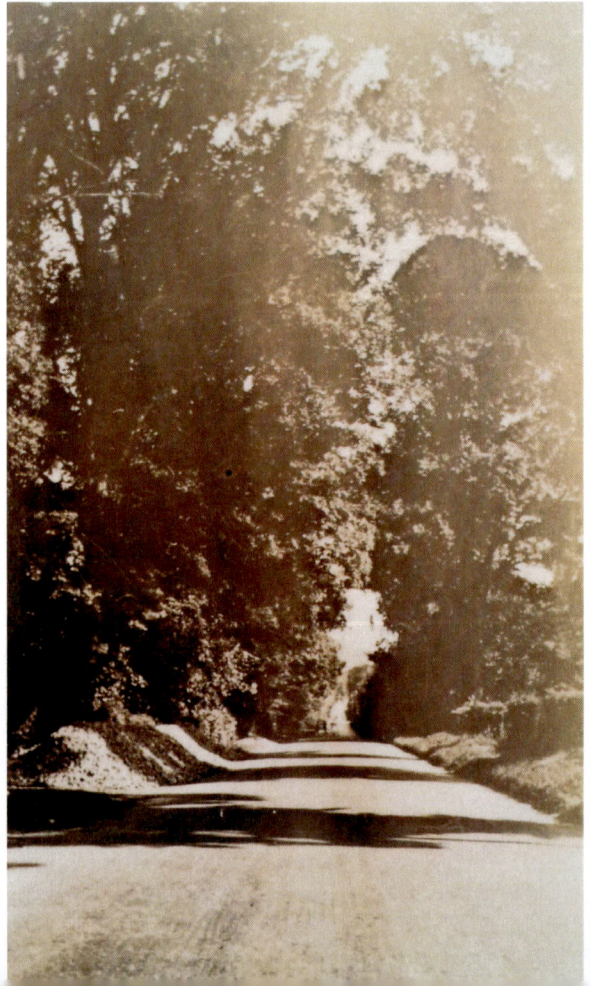

Andrew Wells remembers as a child selling daffodils with his sisters in his field gateway on Seven Mile Lane. He recalls, "My parents were quite happy to let three small children do this, encouraging our enterprise and knowing the road was safe and not too fast." When the M20/M26/A20 junction was built at Wrotham Heath, the road became a fast and noisy transport link with the growing industry of Paddock Wood.

Traffic on the A20

Michael Fuller

When we were kids, especially at the weekend, I can remember a group of us would sit on the side of the London Road at the bottom of Lunsford Lane, simply watching the traffic jam. And this was a continuous queue of traffic from the traffic lights at Wrotham Heath, which is about 4 miles to the west, and past Larkfield, through into Maidstone. I don't know where it finished the other side of Maidstone - but it must have been another five, six, seven miles further on... and this was simply holiday traffic - trippers going to the coast for the day.

Traffic jams usually occurred on a Saturday when people were heading for the coast and then on a Sunday evening when they came back. Maidstone was the main problem. Traffic was at first directed via Aylesford and Bearsted in order to bypass to the town. Then in around 1960, the 'Maidstone Bypass' was built and later (around 1970) the 'Ditton Bypass' between Wrotham and the west end of the Maidstone Bypass. This became the M20.

VILLAGE EVENTS

Cricket in West Malling

Mrs M. A. West

The Horticultural Society flourished for over 100 years and the flower show was held annually on the cricket meadow. (Pitch well cordoned off.) This was well worth going to. The ground would be full of people and the flowers were lovely.

Talking of the cricket meadow, cricket was a big thing in Malling in those days...

I think it was about the 1870's - the Maori team were smuggled out of New Zealand to play at Lords. Such was the esteem West Malling was held in, they also played here.

At the anniversary, they came to England again. By this time we had moved on to Norman Road and the coach carrying the Maori team drew up opposite our house, so we saw them walk back to the field.

East Malling Fetes

John Cook

There always used to be an Annual Fete.

They used to go round house to house through the year and collect money for the fete, and there used to be fancy dress and they used to walk from the top school, right their way down through into the gates into Clare Park. Then they'd give us a shilling, a handful of sweets, and an orange or something like that. The shilling was to spend on the fair. Then they'd have sports where you could win - only pence... but in the running races and all that...

Events in Trottiscliffe

Ann Kemp

Trottiscliffe always celebrates any national event with gusto... all the jubilees and celebrations, street parties and the like - the whole village joins in and celebrates. I certainly remember the Silver Jubilee....

Another event that I think would be nice to mention is... We had, for twenty five years, the same postman in the village - Ray Watson. He was more than a postman... he was a friend to everyone and always, those who needed help, he helped. And when he retired we gave him a surprise party in the village hall and again, pretty much the whole village joined in. It was a wonderful celebration! It was held in January when there was thick snow and people walked across the fields to come and it was a really, really, lovely occasion for a really special man.

> Ray Watson, Trottiscliffe's village postman, retired at the end of 2011.

Knockout Competitions and Netball, West Malling

Betty Honess and Veronica Brimsted

Betty   My ex-husband was the Chairman of the Village Hall Committee, and actually that lounge (in the village hall) is named after him, when it was built eventually. He used to organise the carnivals and Bill Jessop, who used to live at the bottom of Offham Road - he was the one that always worked to do the 'Knock Out' competitions.
It used to be good fun, didn't it? We all played games... You had teams, about eight in a team. And you used to play for a cup and it was only local, but it got quite competitive, actually. It was good fun and it used to be once a year.

Veronica   It was based on the 'It's a Knockout' on the television... You'd have buckets of water the men had to pass over their heads and then move around and then we had the space hoppers and then getting the ball in the hoop and getting the apples out of the water and oh, the crowds!

Betty   Yes! It was good fun to watch and good fun to do.

Veronica   And then in the 70s, we formed a netball club and we did very well. We played all year round. We played in the winter in Maidstone under floodlight and in the summer we placed Medway league and we worked our way from the bottom to Division One. We used to go up into Premier, but we weren't quite good

Ann Turner & Betty Honess as Cooperman & Blunderwoman, West Malling Carnival, 1987

Betty enough to stay in Premier. We'd come back down again, wouldn't we?
And the men played football against us and we made a deal that if we played football, they had to play netball. And sometimes we had the local CID playing netball and football with each other. But it was good fun and the knockouts were really great fun. They really were…

'It's a knockout' competitions ran during the 1970s.

May Day, Offham
Stephen Betts

I remember my father, Stewart, and Uncle, Tony Betts, dressing in chainmail. On May Day they would joust the Quintain. I believe there's a little bit of film in existence somewhere…

It was quite a big event. Sadly it's not done anymore but May Day is still one of the great events of the village!

'The Vikings' Carnival Float, West Malling, 1975

VILLAGE EVENTS

During the Second World War the Quintain was removed, for safety, to Quintain House, as it could have assisted an invading army as a landmark. It was restored to its present place on the Green with much ceremony in the presence of Lord Cornwallis, Lord Lieutenant of Kent on 11 August 1945. A replica Quintain was used in recent years for tilting on horseback during the annual May Day celebrations when the May Queen was crowned, followed by traditional maypole dancing and side shows.

Tilting the Quintain, Offham, August 1976

The 'Quintain' is situated on the Green, a supposedly Roman invention which was popular in Elizabethan times as a means of testing the agility of horsemen. It is said that the Romans left this game of skill behind them when they retreated from Britain, and the name Quintain may have its origins in the Latin Quintus (the fifth), which was used as a first name and also may refer to the fifth road in a Roman military camp, where the Quintain would be erected. The Romans used to practice their skill at charging at the Quintain (or tilting post) with a lance, hitting the broad part of the cross-bar and dodging out of the way before the other end with its heavy weight hit them on the back of the head.

Village Fetes, Mereworth

Alison Lowe and Marion Regan

Alison　　All the village fetes were either at Mereworth Castle or Yotes Court, and they were really very much looked forward to, looking back… those days down at Mereworth Castle. The Robinsons lived there in those days.

Marion　　They were wonderful village fetes. They used to have drum majorettes, and you could run around everywhere - in and out of the pavilions, and I was talking to another friend who grew up in the village and it's one of the most memorable things of the 60s, these wonderful village fetes at Mereworth Castle. It sort of seemed always sunny.

Alison　　And I had to manage the cake stall, I remember - for years! Baking all these cakes and trying to persuade other people to do so. I was quite glad when it came to an end for me! I remember at Yotes Court, it was the Mackays who lived there then. There were stalls for old clothes, and Mrs Mackay used to put her husband's clothes in to get rid of them, and he used to go there and buy them back. It was his favourite jackets and his favourite this, that and the other. She wanted to get rid of them!

And I remember Lady Anne Tree - the Trees lived at Mereworth Castle, and she used to come to church in a cardigan with sort of moth holes. I remember sitting behind her. They were such fun these people who lived in these bigger houses, actually. They were very accessible people.

9 4

Yotes Court.

Yotes Court (listed Grade I), on the western boundary of Mereworth, was built in 1656-8 for James Master, whose descendants, the Byngs, Viscounts Torrington, owned it into the 20th century. It was often let, and in the 1950s was owned by Leslie Mackay and his family. It later became a hotel, but in recent years has reverted to private occupation.

Mereworth Castle (listed Grade I) was a close copy of Palladio's Villa Rotunda at Vicenza and is the oldest surviving Palladian villa in the UK. It was built for John Fane, 7th Earl of Westmorland by Colen Campbell 1722-24; Lord Westmorland also built the baroque and Palladian St Lawrence's Church, probably by Roger Morris, 1744-46. The castle passed from the Fanes through the female line to the Dashwood (Sir Francis Dashwood, Lord Le Despencer, a notorious rake and cabinet minister), Stapleton and Boscawen families. The Boscawens (Viscounts Falmouth) still own the Mereworth estate and most of Mereworth Woods, but sold the castle in 1921. It has had many owners since then, particularly Michael and Lady Anne Tree in the 1950s and early 1960s, and is now [2013] owned by His Excellency Mahdi Al Tajir.

Mereworth castle

VILLAGE LIFE

Addington Play Group

Audrey Reeves

We had a play group in the village for eleven years.

I was more or less bullied into it by my health visitor because I'd been a teacher before and I'd stopped, obviously, to have a family. It was when play groups first started and I actually had it in my house - and my house is still standing! I did that for eleven years and then there were others sprung up around, where they could go.

One of our old farmers, Jock Terry, used to act as Father Christmas and come and give all the children presents. And it was farm land opposite to where I live then. It's now a golf course. And he used to have lambing pens in the corner. And he used to tell me when the lambs were being born so that I could take the children over to see the lambs.

He also had an old ram who was prone to escaping! And he used to find his way to my garden and I used to have to ring up and say, "I've got your ram here".

"Don't let him eat the rhubarb!" he'd say because, evidently, rhubarb's poisonous. And then he'd turn up in his very old Austin seven, and push this ram in the back and take it back to where it belonged.

> Horace Terry, known as "Jock" had a smallholding beside East Street, where he lived, but also rented grazing land beside Trottiscliffe Road. His family has had connections with the village for many years. Jock died in the mid-seventies. Audrey can recall a day in 1969 when the ram came into her kitchen and nibbled at the toes of her daughter, whilst she was sitting in her high chair!
> There is still a pre-school facility in Addington. Sessions take place regularly in the Village Hall.

East Malling in the Fifties

Jean Herrington

Mr Larkin from Diamonds Grocers shop used to come on a Wednesday to take our orders and money. You left the door open and he came in and he delivered the groceries on a Saturday but if you needed anything on a Wednesday he would bring that back and leave it indoors.

When my first daughter was born, all the shops in the village sent something to the hospital, as a gift. It was a very friendly village and they used to have a fete every year and all the children used to go up Chapel Street to the school in fancy dress and walk down to the village to be judged in the park. Another thing I remember is we used to collect sixpence a week for a swimming pool, but I don't know what happened to that because we never had a swimming pool!

It was a very small village then and the Institute used to be the welfare for having the babies weighed and checked. So, you could get to know all the mums. And the children got to know one another before they went to school.

We used to take the children up to a little house up The Rocks for the hairdressers. Mrs Spearman used to cut their hair in the front room of the little cottage.

We had everything we needed in the village then - butchers, bakers... you could call in at the bakers at midnight if you wanted a hot loaf - if you were having a party or anything.

I worked at the Research for a little while before I had my first baby. After that I worked on the fields because you could take the children with you. I worked for Mr Goodwin and he had a coach and he used to pick us up in the morning and drop the

The Post Office, East Malling

children off at school when they got old enough to go to school and then bring us back and pick them up outside the school on the way home. So we knew the children were safe and they were never left, which was very good.

First Impressions - East Malling October 1939

Mrs M. A. West

Now, we were townspeople – London. My father's family had lived in the city and the suburbs for about 600 years. So village life, we knew nothing about. It did not occur to us we would arouse rampant curiosity.

So, after 10 days or so, the squire's sister arrived on our door step to find out "Who we were".

She introduced herself, and proceeded, to question my mother.

Where had we come from, she understood, we had a car? She could see we had the telephone installed. Also, the electricity?

My mother's response (her face rigid with annoyance) was just a civil nod!

But the last question really did the trick... What does your husband do precisely?

One had to be so careful as everyone was related, so witty comments from a 15 year old were not encouraged!

The other thing I remember, all through that winter of '39 and the spring of '40... all through the night, endless trains, going past taking the B.E.F. to France. (British Expeditionary Force).

Foxhunting, Mereworth

Andrew Wells

I remember the hounds meeting at Mereworth, which was a lovely sight, and they had some good runs over to West Peckham, if they didn't get lost in Mereworth Woods. I'm not sure that they reduced the fox population that much, though they were a deterrent, but this has certainly grown in recent years, in line with the

> The West Kent Hunt has not met in Mereworth since its amalgamation with the Old Surrey and Burstow Hunt in 1999, partly due to urbanisation and being crossed by so many roads.

increase in urban foxes – foxes caught in outer London boroughs have been found dumped in the woods here.

Mereworth Well and other Services

Derek Stockton

We didn't have electricity when I moved to Mereworth. All you had was candles, oil lamps or gas. And we didn't have mains drainage then...

And there was no water in Mereworth... I was the only one who had water in the cottages. There was a well, and that was 200 foot deep, and they used to have this bucket on a big rope and wind it up. And washing days, they used to have big baths outside the houses and the men used to have to get the water from the well to tip in the baths so the women could use it to do their washing. And, also, there was an old place with a big copper... and some of the women used to light this big copper up and do their washing. One used to have it Mondays and so on... and then they would change over...

> The provision of mains services to Mereworth was a gradual process. Some of the outlying houses waited several years longer for connection than those in the centre of the village. Installation of mains gas commenced c. 1948, electricity c. 1953, water c. 1954 and drains c. 1960.

Law and Order, Mereworth

Roy Keeler

The thing that I missed most was when the village policeman went. Because, due to my work, I had a close relationship with the village policeman. And a lot of people don't seem to understand how that system worked...

The village policeman wasn't about catching criminals... he was about preventing crime...

And he made it his business to tour the district and talk to people all around, like myself and the farm foreman. He'd say, "Have you seen anything this week, mate?" "What's happening here?" "What's happening there?" And he would piece together where people were poking about, and then he'd go and knock on their door and say, "Look, I know you've been looking at so and so and such and such... If anything happens out there, I shall be down on you like a ton of bricks!" And that's how it was done!

And if you look to the way they look at things now with a tick box system of catching criminals... yes, the village policeman was very unsuccessful... But he was very good at preventing crime!

News, Addington

Louis Fissenden

Years ago if you wanted news, you went to church ... or the pub ... or both. Well, from here, you go by the pub to go to church!

Lou Fissenden who, since the early 1960's has lived in the house on East Street to which his grandfather brought his family from Trottiscliffe in 1902, is right in saying that the quickest way from there to the church is past the pub. A footpath leads to the narrow Millhouse Lane, past the Angel, across Trottiscliffe Road and down Park Road (in the past you had to open a gate here, as this was part of Addington Park). The church path, now a tarmacked drive, then leads up to the small mediaeval church. The Angel was a good place to stop for a pint before heading home for Sunday Dinner. Lou doesn't mention the shop or the school, but that was probably where the women gossiped!

Rock and Roll at the Airfield

Tim Baldock

In the early fifties, the Americans came to West Malling at a base up at the airfield and they were all youngsters, all American squaddies. And they were keen on their time off to get to know the people of West Malling and, as teenagers, we were asked over every weekend to go up. It was obviously a get together, but it was the early days of discos and of course the Yanks had supply flights in regularly and, as kids, we were the first in the UK to hear all the new

rock and roll records... with Buddy Holly, the Big Bopper, Richie Havens. It was super to be part of that pre-rock and roll era before anybody else in the UK got to know about it.

And West Malling was really safe on a Friday, Saturday night, because when they all came down to make use of the pubic houses in West Malling, there was an MP (Military Police) on every corner. So you could let your daughters out in complete safety!

Telephones, Addington

Margaret Castle

And we tried to get a telephone... It was impossible then. You had to go on a waiting list. But we managed to get one and they offered a party line which was quite incredible, 'cause quite often we were listening to each other's conversations, which was quite interesting!

Don and Margaret Castle came to Addington in the 1950's. At that time, telephone service capacity was severely restricted and the Post Office developed a system called a 'party line'. This was particularly used in rural areas. It was a system whereby two or more properties were connected to the same 'local loop', but when a call came in for a particular family, the ring tone was distinguishable. However, if one of the subscribers wished to make an outside call, the neighbour was often already on the line, so he could hear all the conversation. Or the other way around – it wasn't exactly private. Even during the mid-1970's it took weeks for engineers to connect a rural line. Michael and Patricia Richardson remember asking the outgoing occupants of their new home not to tell the Post Office that they were moving, and were thus able to take over the existing line quickly. Otherwise, they could have been isolated down a country lane for a considerable period of time. This was, of course, well before the days of mobile telephones (Also see 'Weather' chapter for more information about telephones).

The Angel, Addington

Audrey Reeves

Even the pub is different now … it really was a village pub … for the locals. On the Green they used to have a sunken kerb with 'Chopper' written on it. It was for one of the 'locals' who used to cut across the green to go to the pub. Rather than him having to step down a high step, they made him a ramp, and that was his route. His name was 'Chopper' Johnson.

The Angel - postcard

The Angel, Addington

Chopper's real name was William Henry Johnson. He was born in Number 1, School Row, The Green, Addington in 1895 and lived all his life there. He did not marry. His mother, Fanny Sparkes, had been born in East Street. Chopper Johnson died in 1980, aged 84.
The Angel Pub has its origins in the late 14th century, and was perhaps constructed by, and to accommodate, the masons who extended St. Margaret's Church. During Chopper Johnson's lifetime the pub had three bars – Public, Saloon and the Snug. The Angel was owned for some years by the Courage group, that had acquired the previous brewery, but it is now independent. It offers meals and accommodation, and remains a central part of village life.

WI Scrapbook, East Malling

Christine Woodger

I'm a member of the WI and a couple of years ago, the WI uncovered the WI book from 1965, about East Malling at that time, in that year.

And there was a lot of discussion about the fact that it'd be lovely to have something up to date and, as a result of that, some members of the 'Craft and Chat' group - some of who were also members of the WI, took it to work on the book throughout 2012 - to have a jubilee book… an up to date book.

This has been a tremendous undertaking… they have worked so hard - taking photographs, asking people to contribute… to compile a record of the different activities that go on in East Malling. So often people say, "Oh nothing goes on in our village", and it's surprising when you actually go through the amount of activities and events that go on in the village… This undertaking is almost complete - it's now a vast book of photographs and a record of the Jubilee year. Everything from the Jubilee picnic that we arranged, to the Queen's Jubilee events, to street parties that were held in East Malling itself, as well as various activities that went on at that time… and it's a superb record. It's at the moment being finished - the members of craft and chat are creating a beautiful cover so that we will have this wonderful record to go alongside the 1965 record - to see how things have changed and also how things are the same… Same complaints about traffic, noise, litter… all sorts of things - you can see in 1965 and again in the 2012 addition.

East Malling Scrapbook 2012

WEATHER

Flooding in Larkfield

David Thornewell

I remember also the floods in the 1960's. The river Medway flooded and the water came up nearly to the bottom of Church Hill. That's the part of New Hythe Lane running down from the church.

The river came all the way up, so the whole of New Hythe was flooded and across the Larkfield side of the railway. And people were wading about down there outside their cottages in wellington boots - it was quite deep!

Flooding at New Hythe from 'Gazette' article published in 1965

and again, Trevor, my husband was away, and I remember hearing on the radio that somebody had been overtaken by a garden shed, and then the radio cut out, and the telephone cut out, and the electrics cut out, and it was very spooky. I remember going downstairs in the middle of night and I'd been working on school papers and I'd had them spread out all over the dining room table, and when I opened the dining room door they were just whisking around the room! It was really spooky, because we've got an inglenook fireplace in that room and the wind would just come down and it just whipped up all my papers and… my heart!

Then we had to cook on the wood burner because we hadn't got any electrics. We did that for a little while and it wasn't terribly successful - grease all over the place! But, of course, I couldn't get in touch with Trevor to let him know what had happened - although I'm sure he was aware at the time.

The funny thing was that the school teacher in the class next door, she was actually due to take some children to a windmill the following day - but obviously that was off!

> The heavy snow experienced in the area was around 1986. The hurricane hit East Malling and the other surrounding villages shortly afterwards in 1987.

Snow and Hurricane, East Malling

Christine Woodger

When we first came back from living in Norway we said to the boys that they wouldn't be able to go skiing because, we just don't get snow like that in England. Then, I think it was the first year… we had so much snow that the school was closed and, in fact, they used their little cross country skis, and I used mine, to get to the bank in West Malling, because we were cut off in Well Street. And a neighbour who, at that time, had a tractor, actually delivered the milk to us because it was so difficult.

Another thing I remember is the hurricane…

The Hurricane of 1987, Addington

Barbara Earl

Then we had the hurricane in October '87… poor Addington was in a terrible state!

I'd ceased being Clerk to Trottiscliffe by then, and one of the Parish Councillors managed to get through to us living here (in West Malling), 'cause they'd no phone lines at all up at Addington. I think Trottiscliffe Road was blocked with fallen trees, and one of the oaks on the green, the one nearest to what used to be the post office - If it hadn't been for the fact that the Parish Council had had Mr R. Hood - the tree surgeon from Loose (I don't think his name was Robin!) - He'd made chains

100

and he'd braced this overhanging branch. That was swinging, but if it hadn't have been braced, the whole of School Row would have gone.

Barbara's daughter, Victoria Hyslop, in St. Vincent's Wood, Addington, after the hurricane

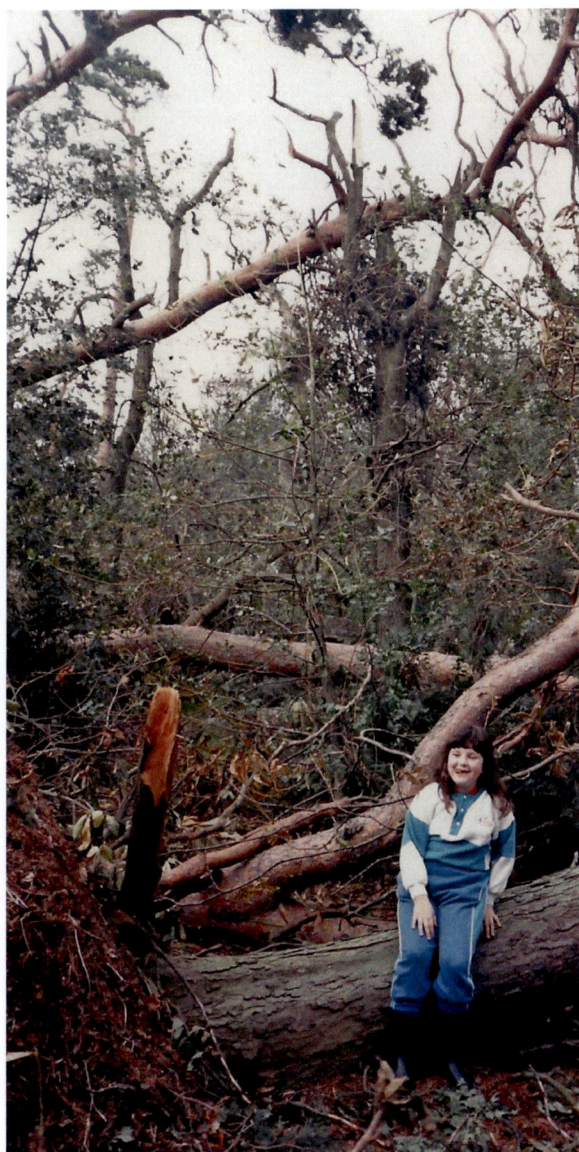

The branches on the oak tree on the Green had to be severely shortened, and the sound of each bough as it dropped to the ground was shattering – apart from shaking the old houses on the Green. Residents were invited to help themselves to any firewood they needed! School Row, the short terrace of cottages closest to the tree, certainly had a lucky escape, though two cars parked beneath the tree were not so fortunate. Since then, the stumps of the limbs sprouted, and a thicket of new branches sprang upwards. The Parish Council has established a long term work programme to keep these thinned and shortened as they mature.

Trees fell all over the village. 'The Angel' was able to keep going, providing hot meals for people, and Sally Ridsdale, of Goodwin's Dairy, Ryarsh, gave outstanding service as she clambered over fallen trees to deliver her milk round. Trottiscliffe Road was cleared fairly quickly, and electricity restored to the centre of the village. Outlying areas were less fortunate – it took thirteen days to get the electricity back on down St. Vincents Lane and, following the intervention of our local M.P., Sir John Stanley, the army was eventually recruited to lift the telephone poles so that, at last, after six weeks, the houses on the lane had a service once more. Patricia Richardson remembers borrowing one of the early mobile telephones (as large as a radio), for the last two weeks – but had to walk nearly as far as the public telephone to obtain a signal!

PARISH HISTORIES

ADDINGTON

Addington straddles the A20 and M20, three miles towards London from West Malling. Its earliest inhabitants built two chambered tombs here, over 5,500 years ago. They are now known as Addington Long Barrow and The Chestnuts and are part of the group known as the Medway Megaliths. The present village was settled in Saxon times and the foundations of its stone church of St. Margaret were probably laid just before the Norman invasion of 1066.

The village lies on green sand, just below the ridge of the North Downs and this light, somewhat unproductive soil meant that the population remained small until the 1920's. It now contains 300 homes and despite being reduced to about 700 acres in the late 1980's. Like its neighbours, fruit, hops and grain were grown and sheep and cattle were raised. A number of businesses operate along the London Road and a substantial sand extraction quarry is divided by the motorway.

A manor house stood beneath the church, owned by a single family dynasty from the 14th to 19th century. The manor had been in the possession of Odo, Bishop of Bayeux and brother of William the Conqueror, who was more of a soldier than a priest, and who rebelled against his brother. It was part of the Honour of Swanscombe (or Talbot Barony) and passed through a number of hands before coming, through a soldier and politician, Richard Charles, to the Watton family. They built the impressive tower of the church and a chapel in which hangs their family memorial with portrait busts of William and Elizabeth Watton, installed in 1652. The male line ended with Elizabeth Watton (d 1775), who married twice. Her son, Leonard Bartholomew, inherited the manor and through his daughter it passed to the Wingfield-Stratford's, who sold the estate in 1887, to C.J. Sofer-Whitburn, a London financier. These names recur in the histories of the other local parishes in this project.

Col. Sofer Whitburn, the son of C.J., was a keen stock breeder and race horse owner, who acquired more land in the district. However, he sold his whole estate at a series of auctions in the 1920's, and in this way, the local farmers became freeholders. Housing development also then took place, both in the centre and along the London Road.

The attractive green, on which the Angel Inn stands, is the centre of a conservation area that includes the church and the wooded grounds of the Seekers' Trust, a community that has lived at Addington since 1933. The village contains a number of listed buildings and monuments. Some of these are on the Green and East Street, others include St. Vincents, Hedgehogs, Westfields Farm, Lane Farmhouse and two homes on Woodgate Road. The church is listed, as are the impressive obelisk, dedicated to the mentor and friend of Nelson, Captain William Locker, R.N., and the finely engraved 18th century chest tomb of a long serving and much loved Rector, standing in the churchyard.

The recreation ground on Park Road is home to a very successful cricket club, recently designated as a QEII field, meaning that it must remain as a recreational facility for perpetuity. The village also benefits from the open aspect of West Malling Golf Club, which is on the former parkland of the manor house. The church is one of the BART parishes (Birling, Addington, Ryarsh and Trottiscliffe).

REFERENCES AND FURTHER READING

Alexander, J. 'The Excavation of the Chestnuts Megalithic Tomb at Addington' in **Archaeologia Cantiana** Volume 66 (1961)

Hasted, E. **The History and Topographical Survey of Kent**. 2nd edition, Volume 4 pp. 542-548 (Canterbury, 1798). Online version: www.british-history.ac.uk

Martin, R. **Trottiscliffe, Addington, Ryarsh, Birling, Leybourne and Snodland Inns & Beerhouses and their Keepers** (Malling Society)

Richardson, P. **Addington - The Life Story of a Kentish Village** (Patricia Richardson, 2012)

Patricia Richardson

BIRLING

Birling lies almost due north of West Malling, on the greensand beneath the North Downs. It is approached from the west via The Street, Ryarsh and from the north and east, the road comes in via Bull Road or from Ham Hill. Ham Hill was part of the parish until the 1980s when it transferred to Snodland. The parish is now long and narrow, stretching from the public open space at Holly Hill down to the London Road.

Like the other parishes in the United Benefice of BART (Birling, Addington, Ryarsh and Trottiscliffe), after the Conquest, Birling was part of the extensive holdings of Odo, the warrior Bishop of Bayeux, who gave it to Ralph de CurvaSpina (Crookback). Unlike many lords of the manor, Ralph actually lived in his manor house, called Comford, which is presumed to have stood to the north of the village, in Paddlesworth, then a sub manor of Birling.

Having passed through a number of families, Birling came into the possession of the powerful Nevill family through marriage in 1435. The church of All Saints, a fine large building standing on a substantial mound, holds their remains since that time in a vault accessed via the chancel. Their first surviving memorial is dedicated to Sir George Nevill, Lord Burgavenny, who died in 1535. It was not until centuries later that the main branch of the family transferred their seat to their other property at Eridge. The church building is mainly of early 14th century construction.

A renowned vicar of 26 years was Rev. Edward Holme. He was an 18th century educationalist who founded Birling's first school on Bull Road, and later opened another at Leybourne. His charity survived for many years and was funded by rents of cottages in the district. Birling school later moved to beside the school, its building is now the Village Hall. Children now attend nearby Ryarsh School.

The village centre contains the Nevill Bull and a number of fine ragstone houses and cottages, many built by the Nevill family. Ryarsh Road and the High Street contain a large number of listed buildings, mainly from the eighteenth century, though some are older. Walnut Tree farm stands on outlying Stangate Street. Fifteenth century Birling Place and its outbuildings are also listed. The "new" manor house on Snodland Road burned down in 1917, but its Lodge and gates still survive and are listed. The area is still actively farmed and a number of businesses operate from redundant agricultural buildings near to the centre of the village. Most of its woodland lies on Holly Hill, an attractive place to spend time. The modern homes in the parish are mainly along Ryarsh and Bull Roads.

REFERENCES AND FURTHER READING

Hasted, E. **The History and Topographical Survey of Kent**. 2nd edition, Volume 4 pp. 474-488 (Canterbury, 1798).
Online version: www.british-history.ac.uk
Martin, R. **Trottiscliffe, Addington, Ryarsh, Birling, Leybourne and Snodland Inns & Beerhouses and their Keepers** (Malling Society)
Wingfield-Stratford, E. *This Was A Man:* **The Biography of the Honourable Edward Vesey Bligh, Diplomat-Parson-Squire** (Hale, London, 1949)

WEBSITES

Lost Heritage - a memorial to the lost country houses of England:
Birling Manor. http//lh.matthewbeckett.com/lh_kent

Patricia Richardson

EAST MALLING AND LARKFIELD

The historic parish of East Malling, renamed East Malling and Larkfield in 1962, as a civil parish stretches from Oaken Wood in the south to New Hythe on the River Medway in the north.

Until the 1920s it consisted of the main village of East Malling based on St. James' Church with separate hamlets of Mill Street around its mill and Well Street, plus the village of Larkfield on either side of the London Road and a large hamlet of New Hythe next to the River Medway with a ferry crossing to Eccles.

The parish can boast the remains of a good Roman villa close to St. James' Church, whose builders utilised its materials in the Norman chancel. The later Saxon history includes the mention of East Malling in the Charter of King Edmund (942 to 946AD), which describes the boundaries of West Malling and a *cwylla*, or well-spring at Broadwater in the south of the parish. Larkfield also gave its name to "Larkfield Hundred", one of the Saxon (and later) administrative divisions of Kent.

East Malling is recorded in the Domesday Survey of 1086 as a manor of the Archbishop of Canterbury, and soon after 1100 the manor was granted to Malling Abbey by Archbishop Anselm. Medieval documents from 1257 onwards testify to the importance of New Hythe as a busy shipping port and shipyard, whilst a rental of Abbey lands in East Malling in 1410 illustrates the importance of the fertile fields to the Abbey's revenues. The manor remained with the Abbey until the dissolution in 1538, thereafter passing to the manorial holders of West Malling between the 16th and 18th centuries.

Within the manor of East Malling, the manor of Bradbourne appears to have been excluded from the   estates of the Abbey, and was in the possession of the Isley and Manningham families from the reign of Henry VIII until 1656, when it was alienated to Thomas Twisden. His descendants rebuilt and resided in Bradbourne House from 1713 to 1937. Part of the Bradbourne estate was sold in the 18th century and in 1793 the Wigan family built Clare House as the centrepiece of a 'new' country seat surrounded by parkland.

The coming of the paper mills at New Hythe began to change the parish from a rural one to one with large resdental areas, with New Hythe hamlet being replaced with industry and new houses built in the 1930s along New Hythe Lane and Lunsford Lane, and to a lesser extent in East Malling.

In the early 1950s the Wigan family sold the Clare Park estate and the former parkland was used
to firstly build Clare Park estate, then Step Stile, Winterfield and Watermeadow. At Bradbourne, Sir John Twisden, a bachelor died in 1937 and the estate was largely taken over by East Malling Research Station.

Meanwhile, in Larkfield, the former Larkfield Farm between New Hythe Lane and Lunsford Lane, including the wood at Larkfield Heath, was developed in the 1960s and 1970s for new houses with shops at Martin Square and another estate now known as "The Trees Estate" on the former land east of New Hythe Lane that once had a small estate based on Larkfield Hall. The M20 and Leybourne Way came around 1970, and the farmland between called "North Larkfield" was developed for more housing with a Tesco Store off Leybourne Way. Larkfield Leisure Centre was built on part of Larkfield Playing Fields which were extended up to the M20. More recently "Larkfield Bank" was agreed for housing and the area north of Leybourne Way, once marshland then gravel pits, became "Leybourne Lakes Country Park" funded by the The Lakes housing.

REFERENCES AND FURTHER READING

Anon. 'Research and Discoveries in Kent' (Report: East Malling Roman Villa) in **Archaeologia Cantiana** Volume 71 (1957), pp. 228-229.

Dudley Ward, C.H. **The Family of Twysden and Twisden**(John Murray, 1939)

Fuller, M.J. **The Water Mills of the East Malling and Wateringbury Streams** (Christine Swift, 1980) see also Wikipedia: East Malling Stream

Hasted, E. **The History and Topographical Survey of Kent**. 2nd edition, Volume 4 pp. 508-517 (Canterbury, 1798).

Online version: www.british-history.ac.uk

Hatton, R.G. & C.H. 'Notes on the Family of Twysden and Twisden' in **Archaeologia Cantiana** Volume 58 (1947)

Martin, R. **East Malling, Larkfield and New Hythe Inns and Beerhouses and their Keepers** (Malling Society)

McNay, M. **Portrait of a Kentish Village** (Littlehampton Books, 1980)

Sinclair Williams, C.L. 'A Rental of the Manor of East Malling, A.D. 1410' in **A Kentish Miscellany**, ed. Felix Hull (Phillimore, 1979)

Sinclair Williams, C.L. 'Maritime East Malling' in **Archaeologia Cantiana** Volume 88 (1973)

Sinclair Williams, C.L. 'The Cwylla of King Edmund's West Malling Charter' in **Archaeologia Cantiana** Volume 89 (1974)

WEBSITES

East Malling Conservation Group:
www.emcg.org.uk
East Malling and Larkfield Parish Council:
www.emandlpc.co.uk
East Malling Research Station (History):
www.emr.ac.uk/history.htm

David Thornewell

KINGS HILL

Kings Hill takes its name from the location on the Chart Hills and their ancient royal connection, called the *cincgesfyrthe* (king's wood or plantation) in the Anglo-Saxon boundaries of West Malling. Part of the king's wood passed to Malling Abbey after the Norman conquest, when nearly 500 acres in the south of West Malling became known as the Abbey Woods. According to the 1840 Tithe Survey, the Abbey Woods were absolutely exempt from the payment of tithes "by reason of their having been formerly part and parcel of the possessions of the Benedictine Nuns of the dissolved Abbey of Malling and enjoyed by the said Nuns at the time of the dissolution of the Monasteries". The woodland remained part of the privately-owned Abbey estates from the dissolution until the early 19th century, when it was sold off to a small number of local landowners.

By the end of the 19th century about half of the Abbey Woods had been cleared for farming, and 90 acres of pasture were designated as an emergency landing ground during the First World War for planes based at Detling airfield when affected by hill fog. The subsequent history of West Malling airfield between 1918 and 1989 is well documented, but can be summarised here as being in private ownership until the Second World War, when it was acquired in 1939 and enlarged by the Ministry of Defence to become RAF West Malling. Between 1961 and 1967 the airfield was taken over by Fleet Air Support Squadrons of the US Navy under NATO, and was then used by Short Brothers for aircraft maintenance and repair. In the 1970s it was purchased by Kent County Council and continued to be used for a variety of enterprises including a venue for air shows before being finally closed in the 1980s.

The first phase of residential and commercial development at Kings Hill, centred on the old airfield, was formulated in 1989 between Kent County Council and Rouse Kent Ltd. With the involvement of Liberty Property Trust the 'new village' has grown to accommodate over 200 businesses and 2000 homes.

The civil parish of Kings Hill was created in 1999, covering 800 acres and incorporating parts of the neighbouring parishes of East Malling and Mereworth, acquired to provide a country park, football pitches and other recreational areas. With flourishing residential and business communities and an ever-increasing range of local facilities, Kings Hill is now about to enter its third phase of development, which aims to add up to 975 new homes and additional amenities to the present community.

REFERENCES AND FURTHER READING

Brooks, R.J. *From Moths to Merlins: The Story of the West Malling Airfield* (Meresborough Books, 1987)

Foreman, I. *A Paragraphical History of West Malling Airfield 1914-1989* (Malling Society, 2004)

Hall, P. *By Day and By Night: the men and machines of West Malling Airfield 1940-1960* (Foxed & Bound, 1998)

WEBSITES

Kings Hill Parish Council:
www.kingshillparish.gov.uk
Kings Hill (News, events, exhibitions, projects):
www.kings-hill.com

Michael North

LEYBOURNE

Leybourne lies just north of West Malling, and its ancient boundaries contained a parish of about one square mile. Its name comes from the little stream running through its pleasant, wooded valley, and it was as *lylleburnan* that the stream was first recorded in a charter of the 10th century. It is also bounded by Addington Brook, and at the time of Domesday contained both a church and a mill. Like other manors in the group of parishes taking part in this project, King William had granted the manor to his rebellious half brother, Odo, but it quickly passed from his hands.

Philip de Leyburn had gained possession by 1166 and it was he who built the castle whose ruins still stand above the attractive small church of St. Peter and St. Paul. This double dedication confirms that this is a very ancient foundation. The de Leybourn family remained lords of the manor until the 16th century and were very powerful magnates, owning large estates throughout the county. Sir Roger de Leybourn accompanied King Richard I to Palestine and took part in the siege of Acre. As one of the rebels against King John, he was responsible for the signing of the Magna Carta. His son, also named Roger, was considered the bravest and most renowned warrior of his day. Sir Roger II took part in the ninth, and last crusade, led by the future King Edward I, in 1270-1271. He was then sent to France as the King's Lieutenant, but died there within the year. He asked that his heart be embalmed and returned to Leybourne. His Heart Shrine is in St. George's chapel in the church. The family became extremely wealthy, but later made their main home at Preston, near Maidstone, the name died out when only a daughter survived, known as "The Infanta of Kent". She left no heirs and the manor and patronage of the church became the property of the Crown. The church then became owned by a London monastery, which held it until the dissolution in 1534.

The castle fell into disrepair and a house was built beside its ruins. The manor passed through a number of different families, including the Levesons, Clerkes and Whitworths. The Golding family of hop fame occupied the house, as did the Goddens, however the early building was destroyed by fire. The current building was constructed in the early 20th century.

In the 18th century Sir Charles Whitworth, K.B., was an envoy to the Court of Russia. With the agreement of his son and by act of Parliament, he sold the manor to the Hawley family, who then built a country seat, Leybourne Grange. They lived there for a number of generations, becoming baronets and intermarrying with local families such as the Wingfield-Stratfords of Addington Park. Sir Joseph, second baronet, restored the church, ran a successful racing stud and built the wall that runs from Pump Close, along Castle Way to beyond Park Road. The pump was installed in 1859 and is now a listed building. The school was built in 1876 by Sir Henry James Hawley. Later members of the family became rector. An impressive rectory was built for Rev. C. Hawley. This is now a family restaurant, with a village hall, neighbourhood shops and a small surgery nearby. His nephew, Rev. Charles Hawley, who died in 1914, was the last of the family to live in Leybourne.

Until the 1970's Leybourne Village was a very small community, with most homes lying beside Castle Way. When a village sign was designed and installed in 1951 an historical pageant was staged by the little school as part of the ceremony, and all the community were involved. However, during the 1970's and 1980's land in the east of the parish was developed for family housing, attractively supported by open public land and recreational facilities. Sadly, the sign was removed due to changes to the road layout. The population grew rapidly and is now about 3,200. This led to greatly increased traffic flows, and a bypass was constructed to take this away from homes. Calming measures were installed along Castle Way. The school came under pressure, so this was extended and a family hotel was later built near to the A20 motorway, lying to the north of the parish.

Kent County Council acquired Leybourne Grange and converted the mansion into a residential home for mentally vulnerable children and adults. A special school operated there for many years, and volunteers supported an establishment for disabled riders. After Leybourne Grange Hospital, by then run by the NHS, closed at the end of the 20th century, the land received planning permission for new housing. The first homes are now occupied and the development is well under way, bringing new challenges to the community, in terms of schooling, health provision, spiritual and leisure needs.

REFERENCES AND FURTHER READING

Andrews, P. (et al). **Kentish Sites and Sites of Kent** (Trust for Wessex Archaeology, 2009) - covering 2005 excavations for West Malling Bypass reported in 'The Missing Prehistory of West Malling and Leybourne':
www.wessexarch.co.uk/projects/kent
Anon. 'Leybourne's Water Mill'.
www.leybournepc.kentparishes.gov.uk (Site pages >History)
Hasted, E. **The History and Topographical Survey of Kent**. 2nd edition, Volume 4 pp. 496-508 (Canterbury, 1798).
Online version: www.british-history.ac.uk
Jessup, J. **Lillieburn to Leybourne** (Jack Jessup, 1985)
Larking, L.B. **A Description of the Heart-Shrine in Leybourne Church** (British Library Historical Print Editions, 2011)
Marlin, D. **A History of Leybourne Castle**: www.dmarlin.com/hawley/docs

Patricia Richardson

MEREWORTH

Mereworth is situated between Maidstone and Tonbridge in a valley through which a tributary of the River Medway flows eastwards. The village is in the Metropolitan Green Belt and contains several Conservation Areas. It has developed on a west-east linear pattern based on The Street, with the other main residential road, Butchers Lane, at right angles to its north. The open aspect of The Street, with houses located largely along the north side and mainly agricultural land and woodland to its south, is a prized feature of the village, in which most houses back onto fields. There are many buildings of historic interest, in particular Mereworth Castle, St Lawrence's Church and Yotes Court, all listed Grade I by English Heritage.

The village's name derives from Mýra'swort, or homestead, and it is mentioned in the Domesday Book 1086 as belonging to Hamo, a Norman nobleman. At that time there were 28 villagers, a church and two mills. Sir John de Mereworth fought at Edward III's siege and capture of Calais in 1347. In the next century the feudal village passed through three great medieval families, the FitzAlans, Beauchamps and Nevills. They owned Mereworth Castle and much of the surrounding area (including Birling) until Mary Nevill, Baroness Le Despencer, heiress to Mereworth only, married Sir Thomas Fane in 1574. Sir John de Mereworth, the Nevills and the Fanes are commemorated in the church in memorials moved there from the medieval church.

The Fanes' descendant, John, 7th Earl of Westmorland, rebuilt their castle in the style of a domed Italian villa in 1722-25, to a design by Colen Campbell, a leading Palladian architect. On a new site further west he built St Lawrence's Church in 1744-46, probably designed by Campbell's assistant, Roger Morris. Both buildings are regarded as among the pre-eminent examples of their era. The church, located on The Street and open every day, has a soaring, eye-catching steeple. Westmorland's heir at Mereworth was his nephew, Sir Francis Dashwood, Lord Le Despencer, a notorious rake, who rewrote the prayerbook with his friend Benjamin Franklin and was briefly Chancellor of the Exchequer. The castle was owned by further Fane descendants until sold in 1922 by Evelyn (Boscawen), 8th Viscount Falmouth. Thereafter it passed through many different hands.

Mereworth churchyard contains the grave of the first person to be awarded the Victoria Cross, Rear-Admiral Charles Lucas. As Mate of HMS Hecla during the Baltic War in 21-22 June 1854, he threw overboard a Russian shell which landed on the deck, saving many lives and probably his ship. He was promoted immediately, and when the VC was instituted in 1856 he was the first to be nominated for this distinction. His captain's wife, also his mother-in-law, was a Byng from Yotes Court in Mereworth, which accounts for his burial here. For many years an annual service has been held at St Lawrence's Church to commemorate Lucas and other winners of the VC. In 2006, the VC's 150th anniversary year, a special service took place attended by Lucas's great-grandson, Michael Adams, his family, the Lord Warden of the Cinque Ports (Admiral Lord Boyce) and descendants of several VC holders with Kent connections.

Although it is still largely agricultural, despite most residents commuting to work elsewhere, Mereworth was long associated with fruit and hop growing. An important hop grower in the 19th century was the Fremlin brewing family, of Herne House, in Butchers Lane. The annual influx of hundreds of hop pickers, mainly from London, ceased in the 1960s as mechanisation superseded them. During the 20th century hops gave way increasingly to top fruit growing, and both have now been replaced mainly by soft fruit. Hugh Lowe Farms, based at Barons Place in Mereworth, is the major strawberry and raspberry grower in the parish and its neighbourhood, and a large local employer.

During the Second World War several doodlebugs fell in the village and the church was slightly damaged. The village played its part in both World Wars, as the war memorial outside the church testifies.

Leisure activities centre on the recreation ground, *The Queen's Head* public house, the *Beech* restaurant, the village hall and the allotments. Fifty years ago there were three pubs, a garage, a post office, a general store and a newsagent and grocery shop. Sports are played regularly on the recreation ground, where the village fete is held each June.

Mereworth Primary School is located at the west end of The Street and was founded as a church school in 1856. The present older school buildings date from 1876.

REFERENCES AND FURTHER READING

Hasted, E., **The History and Topographical Survey of Kent**, 2nd edition, Volume 5, pp. 70-90 (Canterbury, 1798).
   Online version: www.british-history.ac.uk

Martin, R., **Mereworth, Offham and West Peckham Inns and Beerhouses and their Keepers** (Malling Society)

Warren, C.H. A., **A Boy in Kent** (London, 1937)

Wells, A., **The Church of St. Lawrence, Mereworth** (Mereworth, 2012) – available in church

Burke's **Peerage, Baronetage and Knightage and Burke's Landed Gentry** (public libraries and online subscription) – sundry Mereworth families, including Boscawen (Viscount Falmouth), Browne (Lord Mereworth, Oranmore and Browne), Byng (Viscount Torrington), Dashwood, Fane (Earl of Westmorland), Fremlin, Nevill (Marquess of Abergavenny), Stapleton, Tree.

Oxford Dictionary of National Biography (online at public libraries) – covers several historic public figures living in Mereworth (Byng, Dashwood, Fane, Nevill).

Country Life magazine (Mereworth Castle; Yotes Court)

Parks and Gardens website

EH listing details website

Andrew Wells

OFFHAM

The name 'Offham' is said to have Anglo-Saxon origins, deriving from the ham or homestead of Offa. The 'ham' suffix indicates that it was one of the earliest Anglo-Saxon settlements in England.

The settlement developed where a narrow droveway from the North Downs (Church Road) crossed the ancient east-west route (Teston Road) to lead southwards to the Hurst Woods and the swine pastures of the Weald. An important event in the early history of the place is a charter of 833 AD, whereby Offham was given by King Aethelwulf to the Archbishop of Canterbury.

The parish church of St. Michael and All Angels is some distance to the north of the village, which in Norman times was built on the site of a Saxon predecessor close to Offham's two manor houses, Church Farm and Godwell, being related much more to the manor than to the village.

At the time of the Domesday Survey (1086) the village and its lands remained divided between the two pre-Conquest manors, both in the possession of Odo, Bishop of Bayeux and Earl of Kent. Soon afterwards their ownership was once more vested in the Archbishop of Canterbury, and his Tenant-in-Chief was a member of a family which took the name 'de Offham'. In 1313 the two manors were again under separate Lords, and since then the various properties have changed hands many times. However, the manor based on Church Farm remained in the hands of the Tufton family from 1545 until the early years of this century, whilst the small farm based upon the house now known as the Manor House was in the continuous ownership of the Addison family from 1600 to the late 19th century, and this family owned about half the land in the village in the first half of that century.

The best known historic feature of the village and sited on the village green is the Quintain, a Roman invention popular in Elizabethan times as a sporting means of testing the agility of young horsemen and their mounts. Said to be the only remaining example in England, the Quintain consists of a an arm pivoted on the top of a tall post which spins horizontally when charged upon and struck with a lance or staff by the horseman. At the opposite end of the arm is a sandbag which, if he is not quick enough or agile enough to avoid it, strikes the horseman on the back of the head as the arm spins around.

Edward Hasted and other writers of the 18th and 19th centuries described Offham as a lonely, little-frequented place, engulfed by woods and having a gloomy appearance. Today, with very little modern development and a good deal of renovation and conservation of older properties, the place must rank among the most attractive villages in the area, still surrounded by farms and woodland but with the population of agricultural workers and artisans largely replaced by commuters and professional workers.

REFERENCES AND FURTHER READING

Hasted, E. **The History and Topographical Survey of Kent**. 2nd edition, Volume 4 pp. 533-542.
Online version: www.british-history.ac.uk
Johns, F.D. **Some Offham Families and their Memorials** (The Offham Society, deposited at Kent History & Library Centre)
Johns, F.D. 'A Petty Constable's Accounts Book' in **Archaeologia Cantiana** Volume 104 (1987) – the records of an Offham constable from 1814-1822.
Martin, R. Mereworth, **Offham and West Peckham Inns and Beerhouses and their Keepers** (Malling Society)

WEBSITES

Offham Parish Council (Events, Clubs and Societies):
www.offhampc.kentparishcouncils.gov.uk

Michael Rowe

RYARSH

Ryarsh lies just to the north west of West Malling, and until the late 1980's was much larger as much of its land lay in what is now West Malling. The parish then stretched from the North Downs to Teston Road, Offham, and included the area around Ryarsh Lane and Norman Road. It still includes homes on the south side of London Road.

The main village area includes The Street, on which the Wellington public house lies, Workhouse Road and Chapel Street. Roughetts Road, passing the isolated church, then connects to the homes on London Road and Sandy Lane. The village still has two places of worship, the Methodist Chapel on Chapel Street and the parish church of St. Martin, which is mentioned in the Domesday Book. It was originally in the possession of the monks of Merton, so had a vicar, rather than rector, but the Watton family of Addington later acquired the patronage, having bought the small manor of Callis Court (originally named Carews manor after an early owner), lying beside the London Road. It seems that although the village may have surrounded the church during the early mediaeval period, when it was in the centre of the large parish, the Black Death drove villagers away to cluster around their inn. The church was originally dedicated to St. Lambert but, in 1448, parishioners petitioned for the change of name, as the feast of St. Lambert, 12th September, was in the busy harvest period. Coincidentally, the most renowned vicar held this name. Rev. Lambert Larking, who was born at Clare House, East Malling, was one of the founders of the Kent Archaeological Society.

Most of Ryarsh's listed buildings lie in the centre of the village, the largest being Ryarsh Place, built in 1723, owned for some time by the Golding family of hop fame. Cleggetts Farmhouse and some of its former cottages are on Chapel Street. A third inn, the Elm Tree, is now a private house. The Street, Chapel Street, Roughetts Road and Workhouse Road hold a number of interesting houses and cottages, including Victorian and modern homes. A listed mill house and mill race stand behind Ryarsh's second public house, the Wheatsheaf, on London Road.

The village still has working farms, but its sandy soil led to the development of a large brick factory, which operated for many years before recently ceasing operations. Sand has been also been extracted from beneath the Downs, north of The Street. The extensive Ryarsh Wood lies in this area, providing timber for the vicinity over the centuries. A long established bus company has served the village and neighbouring communities well for many years.

Ryarsh has a block of sheltered housing apartments, a large and busy village hall, a separate church hall, a thriving school that has been on its present site since 1940 and a generous sized recreation ground with a much frequented children's playground. The Vicar of the United Benefice of Birling, Addington, Ryarsh and Trottiscliffe, (BART) lives in the Vicarage on The Street.

REFERENCES AND FURTHER READING

Hasted, E. **The History and Topographical Survey of Kent**. 2nd edition, Volume 4 pp. 488-496 (Canterbury, 1798).
Online version: www.british-history.ac.uk
Martin, R. **Trottiscliffe, Addington, Ryarsh, Birling, Leybourne and Snodland Inns & Beerhouses and their Keepers** (Malling Society)

WEBSITES

News and Information:
www.ryarshcommunity.com

Patricia Richardson

TROTTISCLIFFE

Like a number of Kent parishes, Trottiscliffe is not pronounced as it is spelt, but is known as Trosley to local people. The church nestles amongst farmland directly beneath the North Downs and the land of its parish rises to the ridge, the road winding up steep Vigo hill. This was once the main road from London to Folkestone, before the turnpiked A20 was constructed. Two inns, the George and the Plough are located in the village on this route. The ancient trackway now called Pilgrims Way passes through the parish at the foot of the hill. Another former inn, at this junction, is now a private home.

The Coldrum Stones, now in the care of the National Trust, were originally a burial chamber built by Neolithic people over 5,500 years ago and, together with those at Addington, form part of the Medway megalithic cluster. The village is of Saxon origin, already in existence in 788, according to a charter that granted its church to the See of Rochester. For many years the bishops had their country palace next to the church of St. Peter and St. Paul. The village homes were probably next door to this, but moved to their current location after the horrors of the Black Death in 1349-50.

The village still has a rural character, with productive working farms, now mainly growing grain. It contains a large number of listed properties both around the church, such as Court Lodge, built on the site of the Bishop's Palace, and in the centre of the village. One of these is the George Inn and its stables. Amongst others are the wooden clad White House, where Graham Sutherland lived for many years, Great Reeds, Gore Cottage and Long Gore, Rouse's Farm, formerly the Tanyard, and the Forge. Further out are Miller's Farmhouse with its surrounding listed barns and Little Commority on Pilgrims Way.

As agricultural practice changed after two world wars, agricultural buildings, especially oasts, became family homes. The village centre also includes a number of pleasant modern homes, a primary school, a much used village hall and a recreation ground with tennis courts. Further afield, Trosley Country Park on the chalk downland above the village provides residents and visitors with 160 acres of grassland and woodland offering spectacular views to the Weald in the south. The Park has been designated a Site of Special Scientific Interest where careful management has encouraged the return of rare flora and fauna.

REFERENCES AND FURTHER READING

Hasted, E. **The History and Topographical Survey of Kent**. 2nd edition, Volume 4 pp. 549-555 (Canterbury, 1798).
Online version: www.british-history.ac.uk
Martin, R. **Trottiscliffe, Addington, Ryarsh, Birling, Leybourne and Snodland Inns & Beerhouses and their Keepers** (Malling Society)

WEBSITES

News and Information:
www.trottiscliffe.org.uk

Patricia Richardson

WEST MALLING

The manor of West Malling was granted to Bishop Buhric of Rochester by King Edmund (942-46), appropriated by Bishop Odo of Bayeux as Earl of Kent after the Norman conquest and recovered for the bishopric at the Penenden Heath trial a decade later. At the Domesday Survey in 1086 West Malling boasted a church and a mill but few inhabitants. At this time the main focus of settlement was the early Norman chapel of St. Leonard which stood at the roadside springhead below St. Leonard's Tower - the more durable remains of Bishop Gundulf's estate centre known historically as the Precinct or Borough of Ewell.

The town was established in the early 12th century following Gundulf's foundation of Malling Abbey in 1090 and a grant of Saturday markets and other privileges by King Henry I. To accommodate the markets the present High Street was created by widening a section of a drove road between the Wealden dens and settlements in the lower Medway Valley. With the provision of a new church (St. Mary the Virgin) and the allocation of burgage plots to Abbey tenants, a lasting template was established for medieval development in and around the High Street. The survival of a mix of buildings from all periods between the 12th and 19th centuries, together with a study of medieval records and property boundaries, suggest that the early 12th century town plan has been preserved to the present day.

Some residential expansion of West Malling started with the building of New Town in the Norman Road/Alma Road area between the 1880s and the early 1900s, then separated from the old town by fields. By 1908 further developments followed in Teston Road, Church Fields, Ryarsh Lane, Town Hill and London Road. Some infilling occurred in the inter-war years, but the most significant expansion took place with the development of the Fartherwell Estate in the 1950s and 1960s, covering some 30 acres to the west of Teston Road.

Following the dissolution of the Abbey in 1538 the town continued to thrive as a market centre for livestock fairs, agricultural produce and local industry until the early 20th century. Despite the closure of the Saturday market in the 18th century, some of the spirit of earlier times has now been recaptured with the introduction of a monthly farmers' market.

The town, where the first recorded cricket match in Kent was played in 1705, has also been regarded as a picturesque attraction by many notable visitors including Dr. Samuel Johnson and the artists J.M.W. Turner and John Downman.

The present town continues to attract artists, tourists, shoppers and diners, house-hunters, business entrepreneurs and Abbey visitors on retreat, whilst the residents benefit from a wide range of facilities including schools, churches, health care, railway and bus services, a public library, public open spaces and several clubs and societies covering a range of sports, hobbies and other interests.

While the civil parish of West Malling remains mainly rural and agricultural in character, almost 30% of the original area has been lost to the creation of Kings Hill parish in 1999.

REFERENCES AND FURTHER READING

Cronk, A. **A Short History of West Malling, Kent** (Anthony Cronk, 1951)
Fielding, C.H. **Memories of Malling and its Valley** (Henry C.H. Oliver, 1893)
Hasted, E. **The History and Topographical Survey of Kent.** 2nd edition, Volume 4 pp. 518-533 (Canterbury, 1798).
Online version: www.british-history.ac.uk
Lawson, A.W. **A History of the Parish Church of St. Mary the Virgin, West Malling** (Henry C.H. Oliver, 1904)
Malling Abbey. **Living Stones: The Story of Malling Abbey** (Malling Abbey, 2005)
Martin, R. (ed.) **West Malling Tithe Apportionments,** 1840 (Malling Society - CD)
Martin, R. **West Malling Inns and Beerhouses and their Keepers** (Malling Society, 2009)
North, M. 'St. Leonard's Tower: Some Aspects of Anglo-Norman Design and Construction' in **Archaeologia Cantiana** Volume 121 (2001)
Oakley, A. **Malling Abbey 1090-1990** (Malling Abbey, 1990)
Tatton-Brown, T. 'The Buildings of West Malling Abbey' in **Architectural History** Volume 44 (2001)
Womens' Institute. West **Malling WI Scrapbook** (Foxed & Bound, 1999)

BIBLIOGRAPHY

WEBSITES

West Malling Parish Council:
www.westmallingpc.kentparishes.gov.uk
Malling Photographic Society:
www.mallingphotographicsociety.org
Malling Society: www.themallingsociety.org.uk
Malling Union Workhouse:
www.workhouses.org.uk/malling
Music @ Malling Festivals:
www.musicatmalling.com
Malling Art Club:
www.mallingartclub.co.uk
Malling Action Partnership:
www.sca21.wikia.com/wiki/Malling_Action_Partnership
West Malling Resource Centre:
www.west-malling.co.uk

Michael North

The following list is intended to provide a basis for the study of Kentish History beyond the context of the individual Parish. Most of the printed books listed are available through the Kent Library Services or held in the reference collection at the Kent History and Library Centre, Maidstone. Additional information has been added for Internet sources where available.

General, Topograhical and Social History:

Everitt, **A. Continuity and Colonization** (Leicester University Press, 1986)

Hasted, E. **The History and Topographical Survey of Kent**, Volume IV (Second edition, 1798).
- Complete online version (12 volumes): www.british-history.ac.uk

Lambarde, W. **A Perambulation of Kent** (1570; reprinted 1826)

Lawson, T. &Killingray, D. (eds.). **An Historical Atlas of Kent** (Phillimore, 2004)

Morgan, P. (ed.). **Domesday Book: Kent** (Phillimore, 1983)

Ogley, B. Kent, **A Chronicle of the Century** in 4 Volumes: 1900-1924, 1925-1949, 1950-1974, 1975-1999 (Froglet Press, 1996-99)

Whitney, K.P. **The Kingdom of Kent** (Phillimore, 1982)

Architecture:

English Heritage: The National Heritage List for England:
www.english-heritage.org (Search your Town or Parish from the National Heritage List)

Newman, J. **The Buildings of England**: West Kent and the Weald (Yale, 2012)

Listed Buildings:
www.britishlistedbuildings.co.uk/england/kent (Search by Parish)

Thorpe, J. (Junior) **Antiquities in Kent, Within the Diocese of Rochester** (London, 1788)

Archaeology:

Jessup, R. Ancient People and Places Series: **South-East England** (Praeger USA, 1970)

Philp, B. & Dutto, M. **The Medway Megaliths**, 3rd Edition (Kent Archaeological Trust, 2005)

Williams, J.H. (ed.) **The Archaeology of Kent to AD 800** (Boydell Press & KCC, 2007)

HISTORICAL RESEARCH: RESOURCES IN KENT

Kent History and Library Centre, Maidstone (previously Centre for Kentish Studies) preserves a wide range of original documents from the early Anglo-Saxon period to the twentieth century, including estate maps, property sale catalogues, photographs, parish records and family collections. Note that the archives contain many more items than are currently listed on the Kent History website. Intending users should contact the Centre for more detailed information before visiting: www.kentarchives.org.uk

Other Archives/Repositories in Kent

Canterbury Cathedral Archives, The Precincts, Canterbury CT1 2EH:
www.canterbury-cathedral.org/conservation/archives

Kent Archaeological Society (see website for scope and membership):
www.kentarchaeology.org.uk

Malling Society (Freda Barton collection of photographs & Heritage Centre):
www.themallingsociety.org.uk

Medway Archive and Studies Centre, Civic Centre, Strood ME2 4AU (includes Rochester Cathedral Archives):
www.medway.gov.uk

Snodland Millennium Museum, Waghorn Road, Snodland:
www.snodlandhistory.org.uk

Michael North

PHOTOGRAPH AND ILLUSTRATION CREDITS

COVER
(Listed left to right, top to bottom)

Larkfield Village Sign *(The Beat Project)*

East Malling. *Courtesy of East Malling Conservation Group*

Homefront bus at Ryarsh School celebrations. *Courtesy of Ryarsh Primary School*

Leybourne Lakes Country Park *(The Beat Project)*

Trottiscliffe *(The Beat Project)*

Cottage in Birling. *Courtesy of Margaret Ivell*

Memorial, Kings Hill. *(The Beat Project)*

Crossroads, Mereworth. *Courtesy of Martin Willgoss*

Making up the road round Addington Green, 1967. *Courtesy of Patricia Richardson*

Four Generation, Briggs Family. *Courtesy of Tony Briggs*

'Skis' at Offham May Day. *Courtesy of M D Rowe*

Hope Statue, West Malling. *(The Beat Project)*

AGRICULTURE
Church Farm, 1932. *Courtesy of Stephen Betts*

Hop Picking at Aldon Farm, 1912. *Courtesy of J. B. Lander*

Sheep at Church Farm, 1956. *Courtesy of Stephen Betts*

Women's Land Army and Timber Corps badge awarded in 2008. *Courtesy of Stuart A. Olsson*

CHURCH
Holy Trinity Church, Larkfield *(The Beat Project)*

Leybourne Church, 1997. *Courtesy of Bob Clarke.*

Reverend Bone and Cyril Botteril putting the new weather vane on Ryarsh Church, 1968. *Courtesy of Brenda Botteril.*

St. Mary's Abbey, 12th century Norman Tower and Guesthouse. *Courtesy of Malling Abbey*

COMMUNITY PROJECTS AND AMENITIES DEVELOPMENT
Comp Farmhouse. *Courtesy of F D Johns (decd.)*

First Match of Addington Cricket Club, 1959. *Courtesy of Peter Robinson*

DEVELOPMENTS – HOUSING AND INFRASTRUCTURE
Leybourne Lakes Country Park *(The Beat Project)*

Mike Rowe and family at 'The Great Warbirds Air Display' in 1983. *Courtesy of M D Rowe*

EARLY MEMORIES

Birling Manor after the fire. *Courtesy of Maureen Balfour (decd.)*

Fartherwell Hall. *Courtesy of Stephen Betts*

High Street, West Malling. Photo taken by Freda Barton, *courtesy of The Malling Society*

St. Martin's Square, Larkfield *(The Beat Project)*

West Malling Fire Station circa 1898. *Courtesy of Mike North*

EDUCATION
Children hiding under their desks, 70th Anniversary Celebrations at Ryarsh School. *Courtesy of Ryarsh Primary School.*

Louise Parfitt, 70th Anniversary Celebrations at Ryarsh School. *Courtesy of Ryarsh Primary School.*

Manningham House, Infants School, East Malling, 1965. *Courtesy of East Malling Conservation Group*

Mereworth School, 1931. *Courtesy of Martin Willgoss*

Mr Rabjohn's class of 1959, Chapel Street School, East Malling. *Courtesy of D Rabjohn*

Offham School. *Courtesy of Stephen Betts*

West Malling Boys School, circa 1919. *Courtesy of Tony Briggs*

HISTORICAL BUILDINGS AND SITES OF INTEREST
Baldocks, West Malling. *Courtesy of Photo taken by Freda Barton, courtesy of The Malling Society*

Malling Heritage Centre Plaque. *(The Beat Project)*

The Chestnuts Neolithic Tomb, Addington taken in 2003. *Courtesy of Joan Bygrave*

The Memorial outside the Kings Hill Community Centre. *Courtesy of D Murray*

Trosley Towers Bridge. *Photo taken in April 2009 courtesy of Mike Towler*

PHOTOGRAPH AND ILLUSTRATION CREDITS

Tunnel at Malling Abbey. *Courtesy of Mike North*

HISTORY DISCOVERED
Newspaper article, Offham Shooting. *Courtesy of Syd and Jo*

The Red Lion, Offham. *Courtesy of F D Johns (decd.)*

Thomas Augustus Douce Esq. Painted by John Downman. *Courtesy of Molly Potts*

LOCAL BUSINESSES AND EMPLOYMENT
Arthur Briggs's Bread Cart, 1915. *Courtesy of Tony Briggs*

Function at 'Greenways'. *Courtesy of David Cameron*

Linda Javens at Reeds and Cobdown Sports Day. *Courtesy of Linda Javens*

Planting Rootstocks at East Malling Raymar Cinema *courtesy of West Malling W.I.*

Research Station. *Courtesy of EMRS*

Symonds Bakery. *Courtesy of Courtesy of East Malling Conservation Group*

PUBLIC LIFE
Leybourne Castle. *Courtesy of Maureen Balfour (decd.)*

The 'Hope' Statue, West Malling. *(The Beat Project)*

West Malling Farmers' Market. *(The Beat Project)*

West Malling Courthouse, 1985. *Courtesy of M D Rowe*

SIGNIFICANT PEOPLE AND VISITORS
Addington Vale. *Courtesy of Patricia Richardson*

Delivery Bikes outside Mr. Gould's Shop, 1935. *Courtesy of Martin Willgoss*

Dr. Who at the Addington Sand Quarry. *Courtesy of Joan Bygrave*

Mr. Hook, Mr. Boorman and Mr. Watts at Mereworth Garage. *Courtesy of Martin Willgoss*

The Collins Sisters with Fred and Margaret Gandon (in pink). *Courtesy of Linda Javens*

Trottiscliffe Village Sign. *(The Beat Project)*

THE IMPACT OF WAR
Addington Church, 1939. *Courtesy Patricia Richardson*

Tony Briggs (second from left) with family, Peace Day Celebrations 1945. *Courtesy of Tony Briggs*

Paddlesworth Farm. Image taken from post card originally produced and sold by Hanbrooks of Snodland circa, *courtesy of Trevor Lingham*

VAD Hospital, Malling Area. *Courtesy of East Malling Conservation Group*

Woolwich Central School evacuees outside

TRANSPORT
Bull Road, Birling. *Courtesy of Courtesy of Maureen Balfour (decd.)*

Offham Level Crossing, 1966. *Courtesy of Cyril Botteril (decd.)*

Seven Mile Lane. *Courtesy of Martin Willgoss*

VILLAGE EVENTS
Ann Turner & Betty Honess as Cooperman & Blunderwoman, West Malling Carnival, 1987. *Courtesy of Betty Honess*

Mereworth Castle c 1760. *Courtesy of Andrew Wells*

'The Vikings' Carnival Float, West Malling, 1975. *Courtesy of Betty Honess*

Tilting the Quintain, Offham, August 1976. *Courtesy of M D Rowe*

Yotes Court. *Courtesy of Andrew Wells*

VILLAGE LIFE
East Malling Scrapbook 2012. *(The Beat Project)*

The Angel, Addington *(The Beat Project)*

The Angel Pub postcard. *C ourtesy of Patricia Richardson*

The Post Office, East Malling. *Courtesy of East Malling Conservation Group*

WEATHER
Flooding at New Hythe from 'Gazette'article published in 1965. *Courtesy of David Thornewell*

Victoria Hyslop in St. Vincent's Wood, Addington, after the hurricane. *Courtesy of Patricia Richardson*